Stefan Draschan
Double Take

STEFAN DRASCH AN DOUBLE TAKE

Text by | *Text von*
Barbara Hess

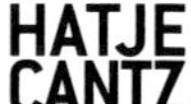

CARS MATCHING HOMES

2015–2023

One meaning in German for "double take" refers to a retarded ignition, a technical phenomenon from the world of combustion engines that is gradually disappearing. It is only at second glance that the correspondences between the buildings and the vehicles parked in front of them become apparent—aesthetic effects reminiscent of camouflage.

Eine mögliche Übersetzung für „double take" ist „Spätzündung" – ein technisches Phänomen aus der Welt der Verbrennungsmotoren, die im Verschwinden begriffen ist. Erst auf den zweiten Blick zeigen sich Korrespondenzen zwischen Bauwerken und den vor ihnen geparkten Fahrzeugen – ästhetische Effekte, die an Camouflage erinnern.

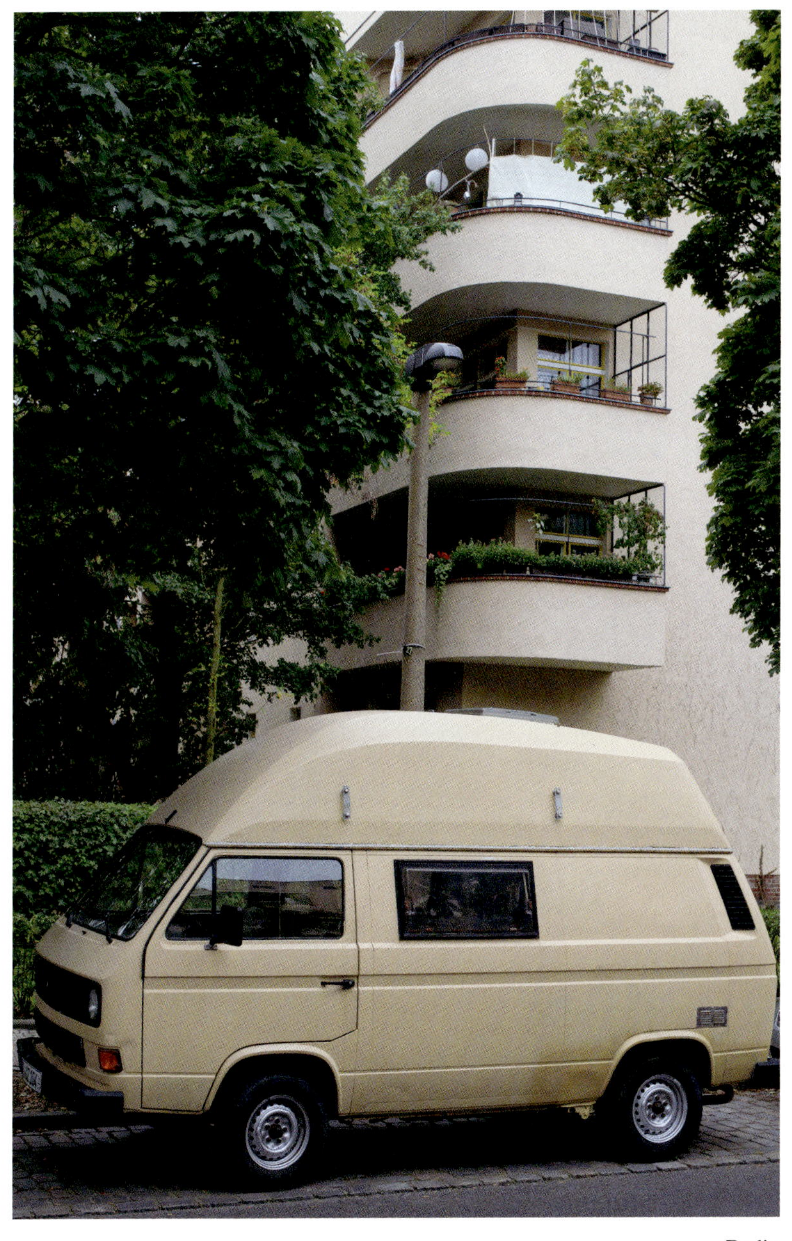

Berlin

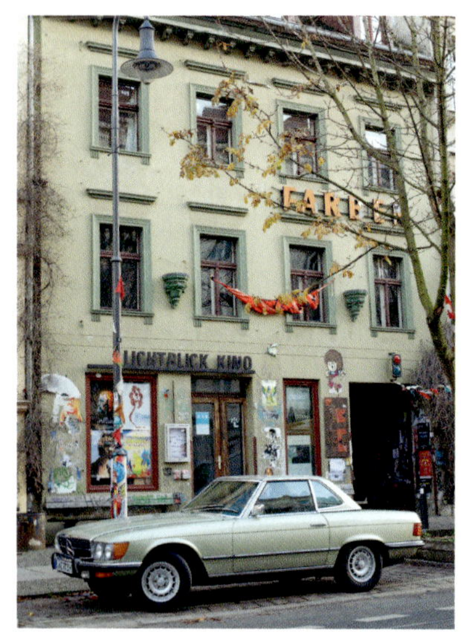

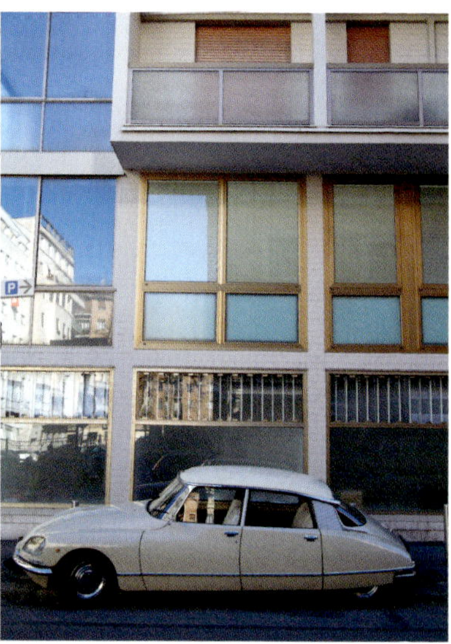

Berlin | Milan

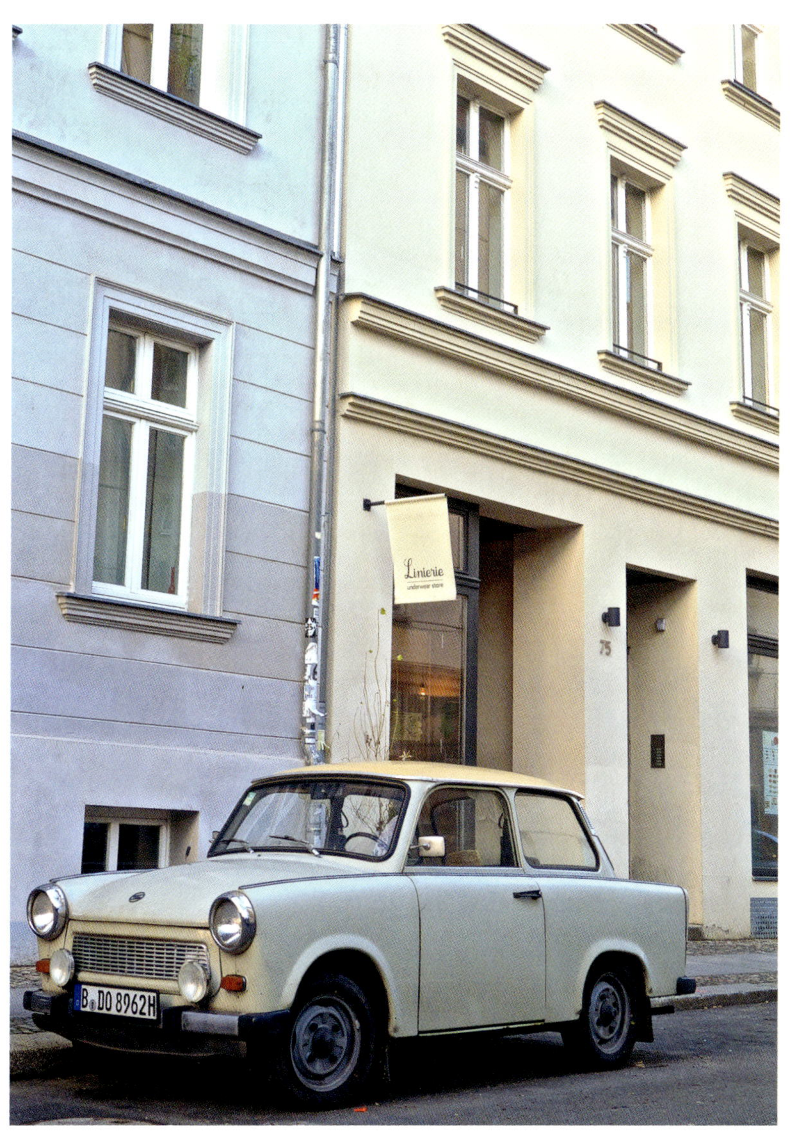

Berlin

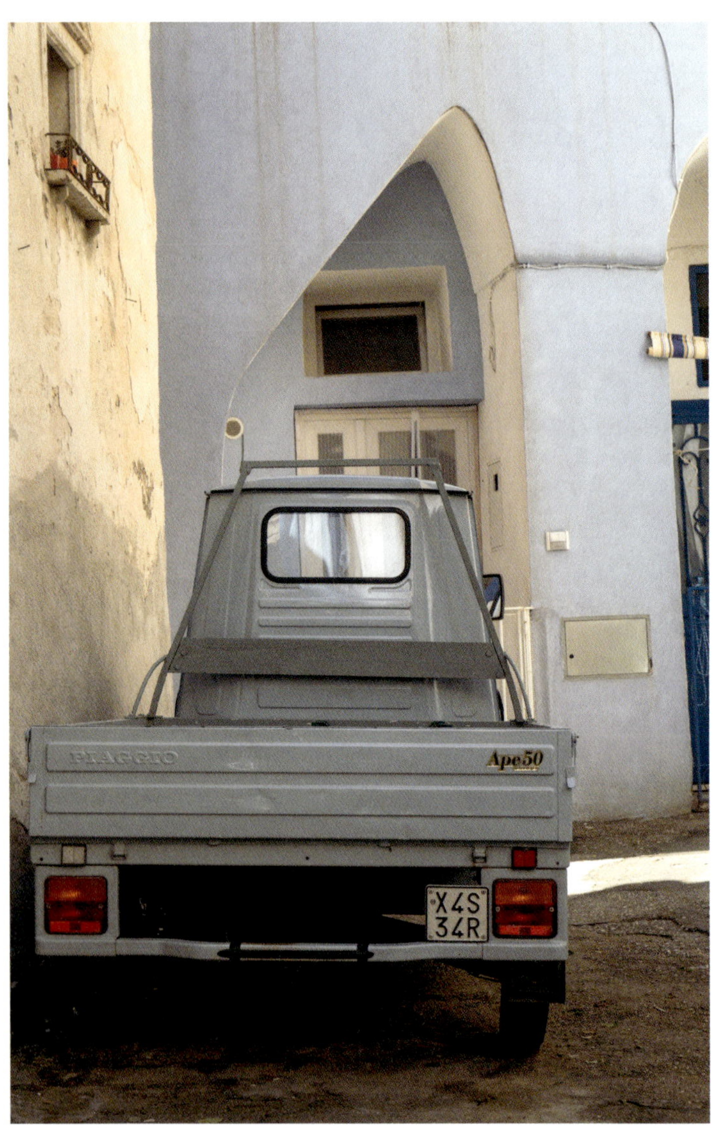

Procida

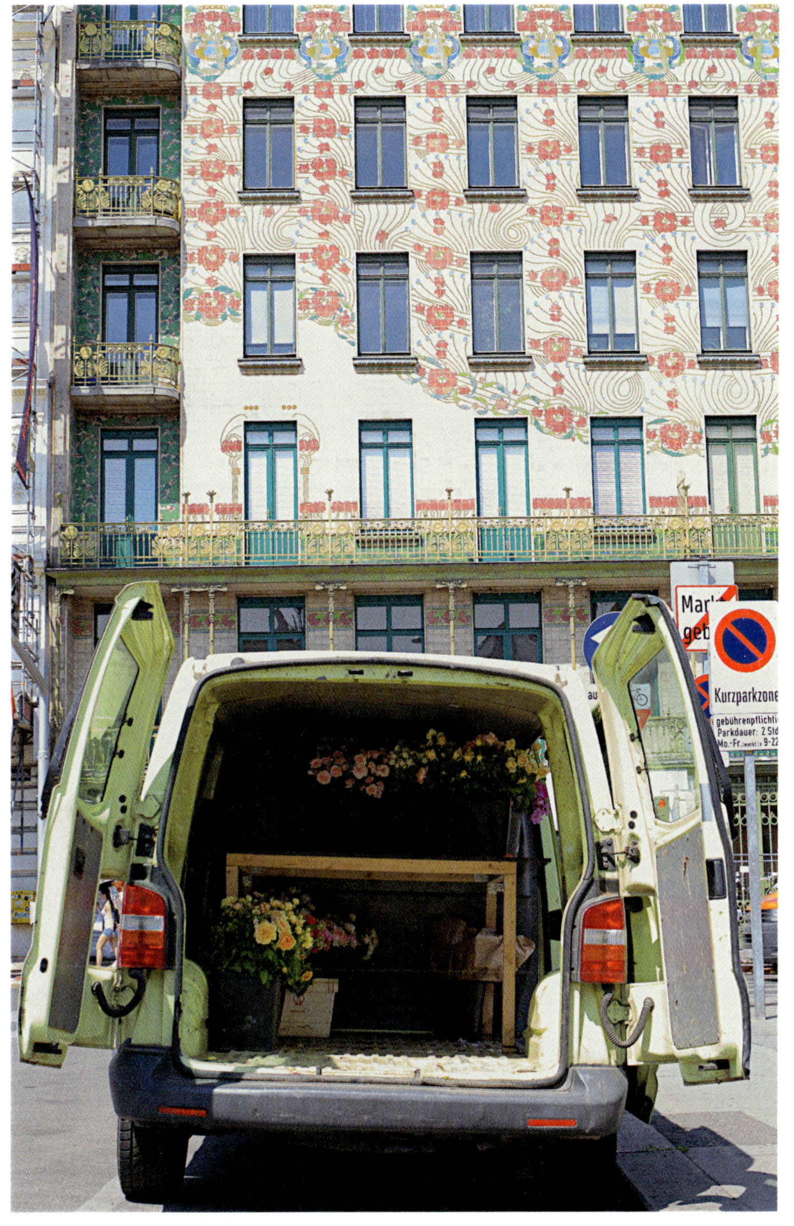

Vienna

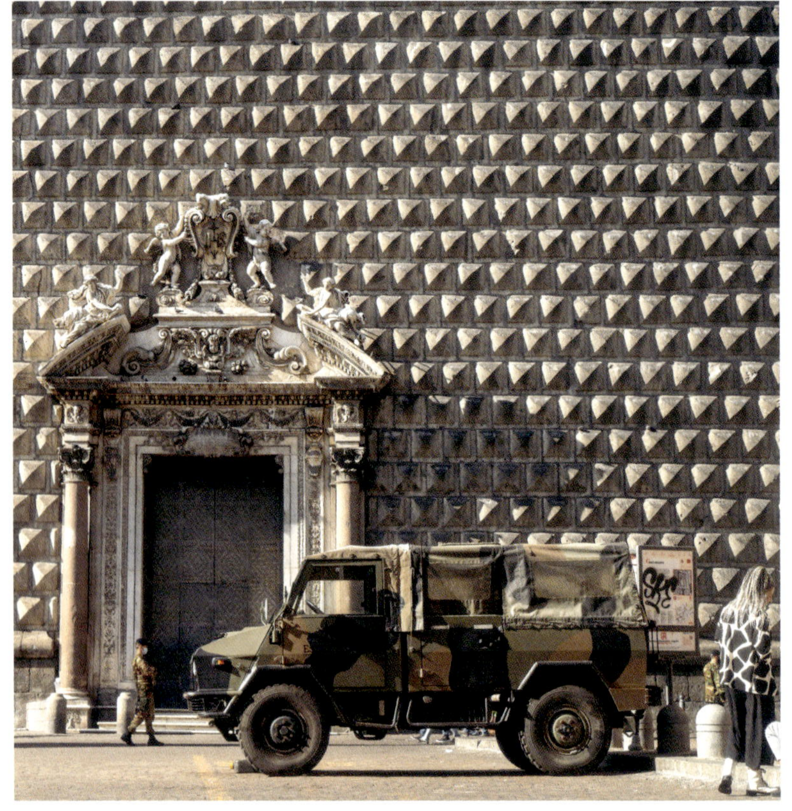

Naples

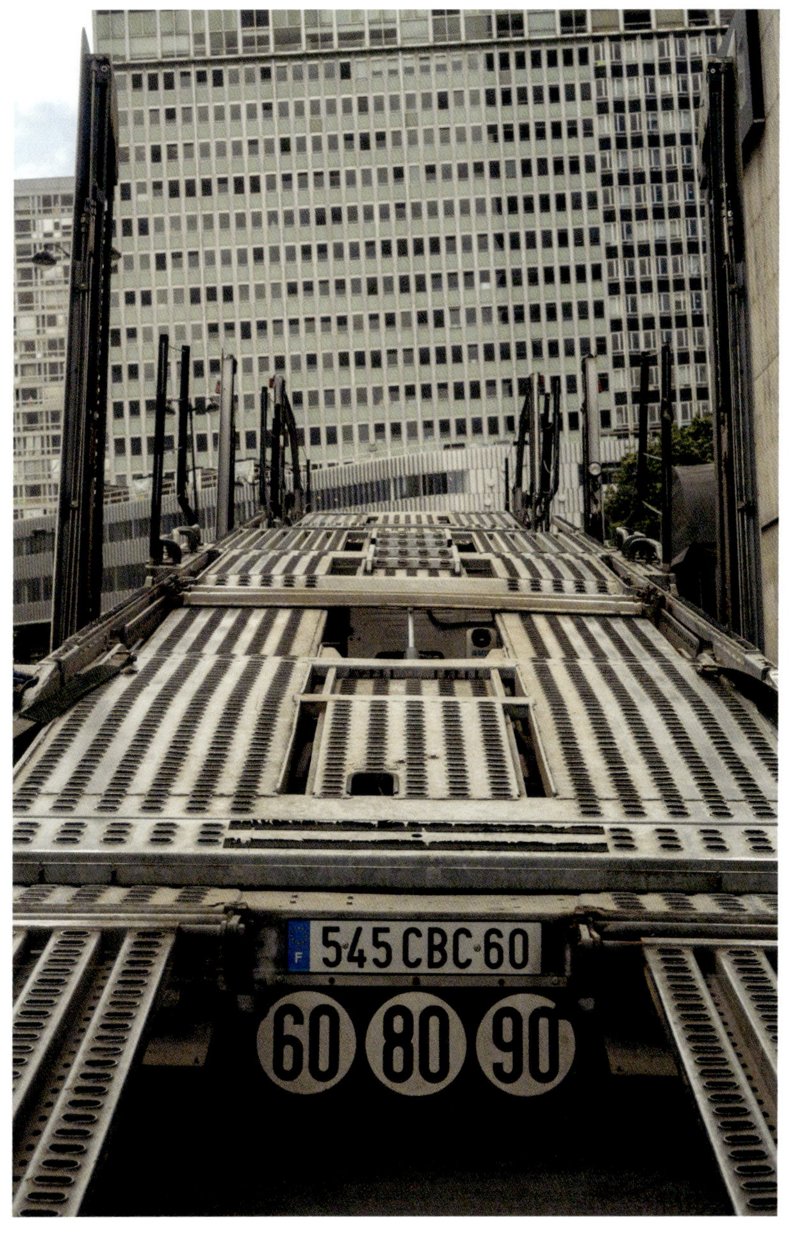

Paris

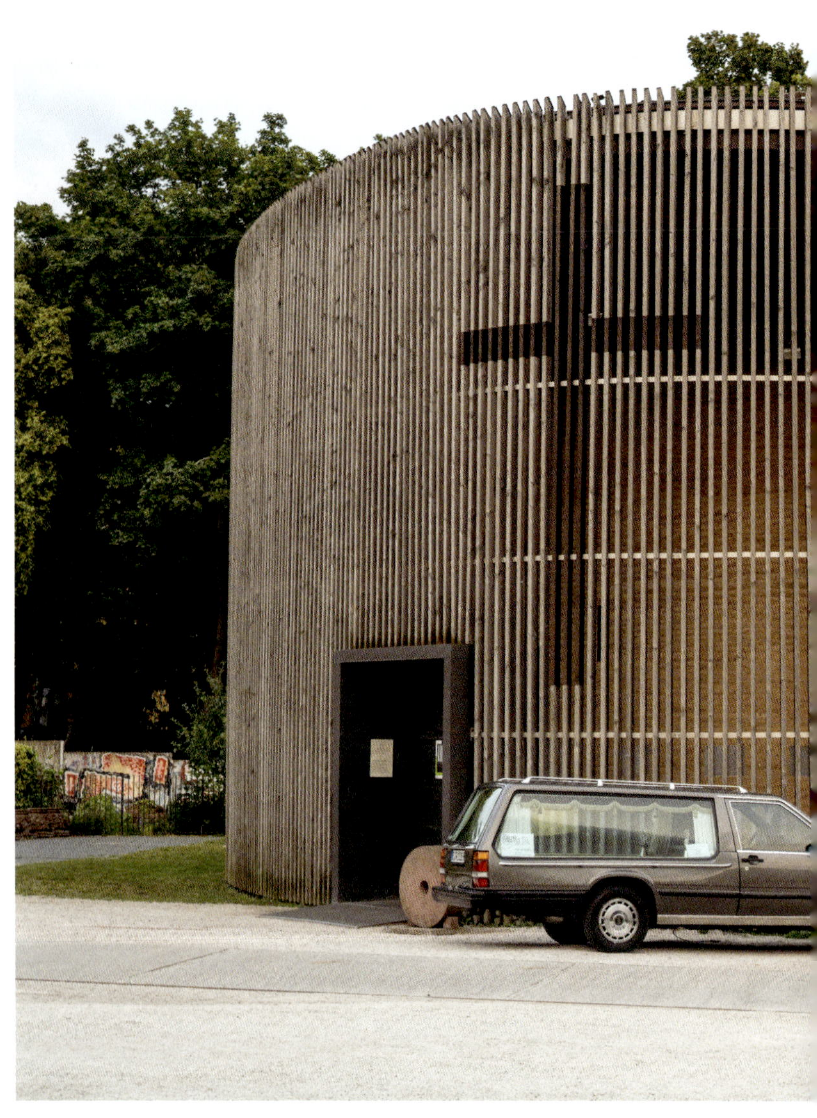

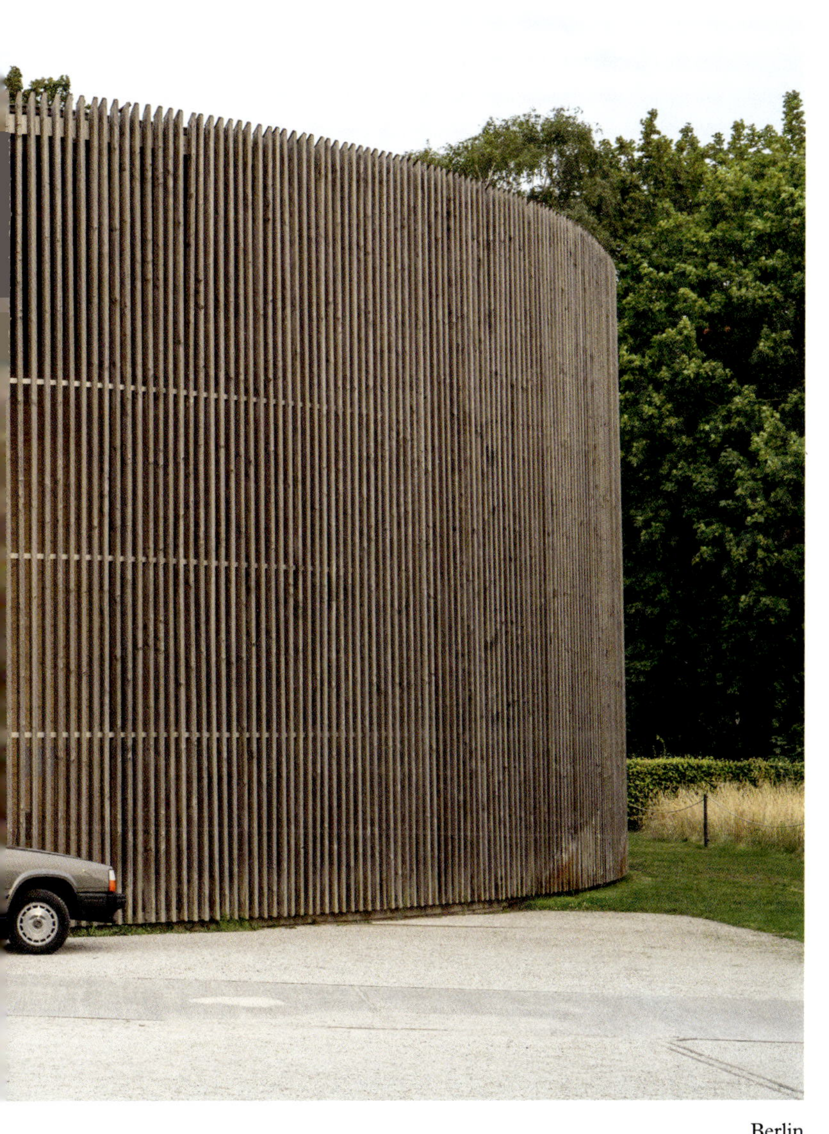

Berlin

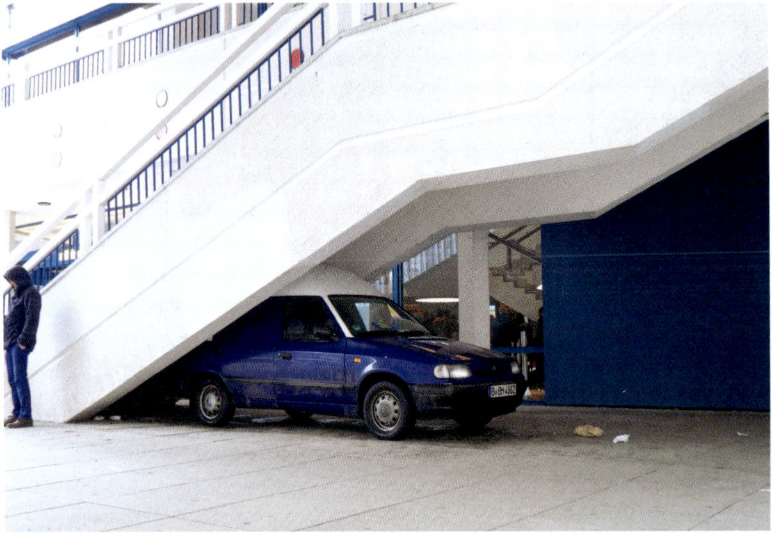

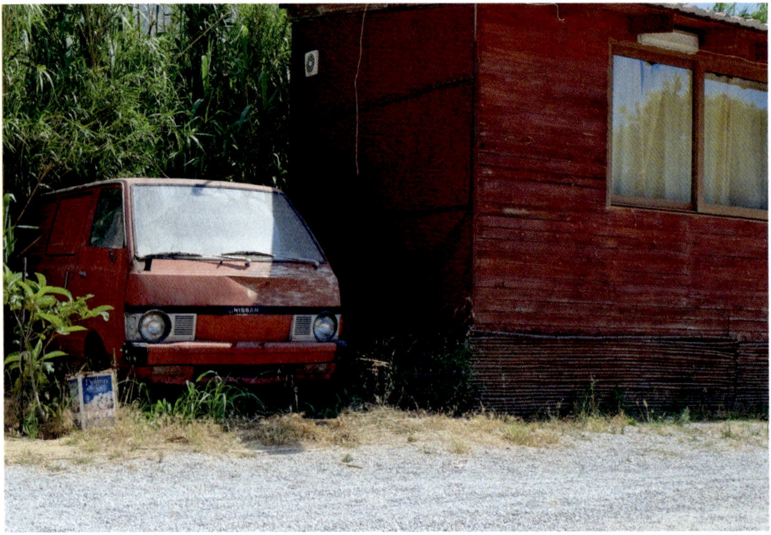

Berlin | Crete

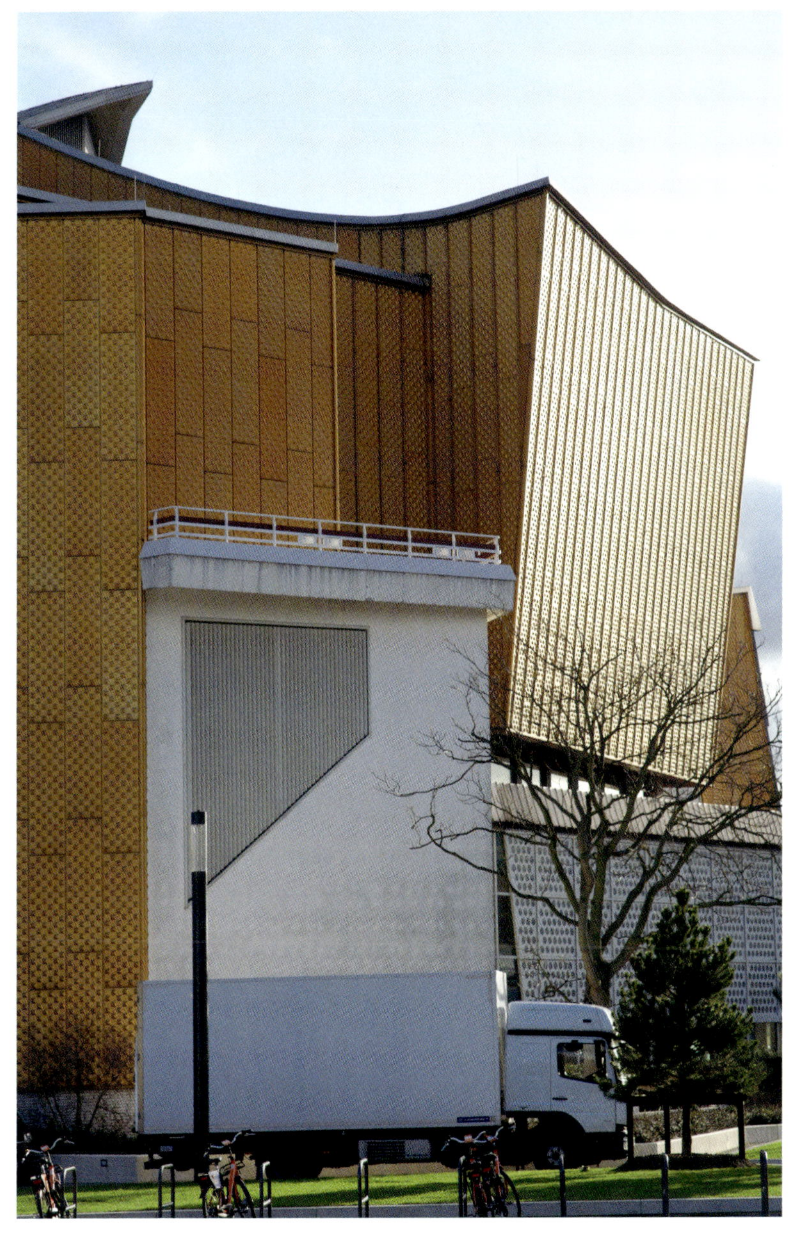

Berlin

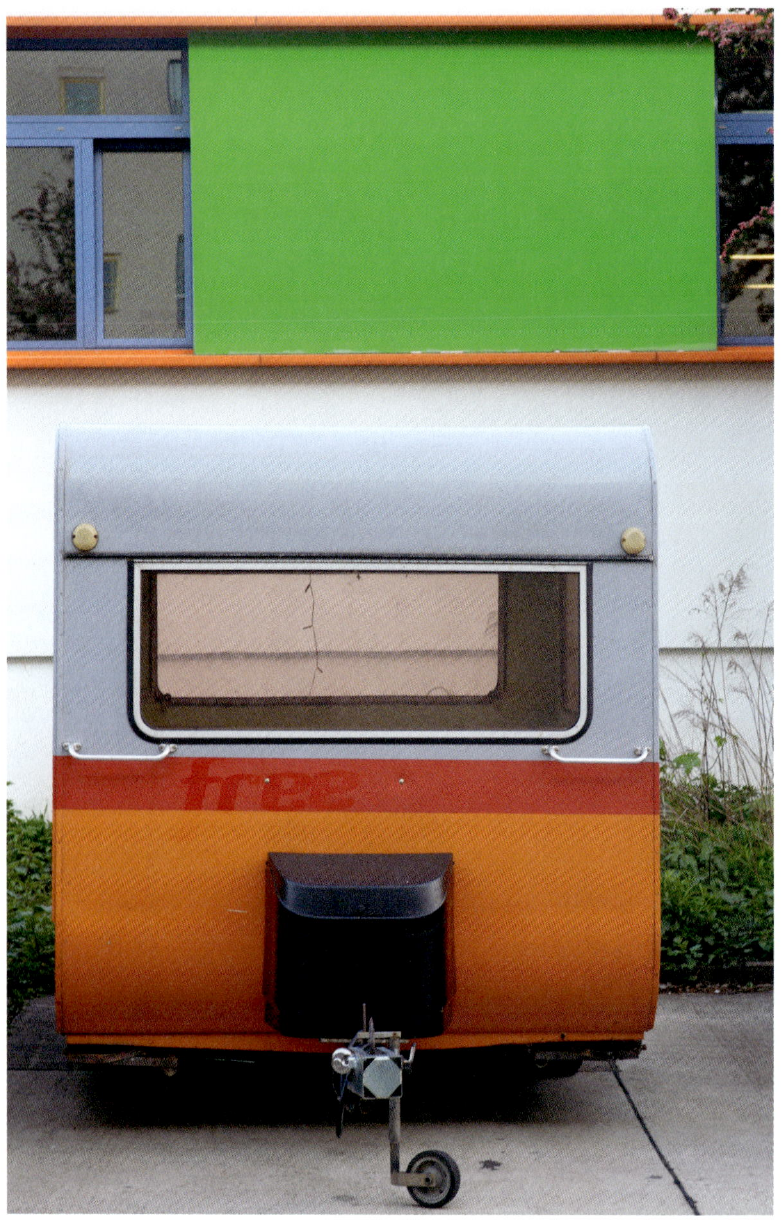

Berlin

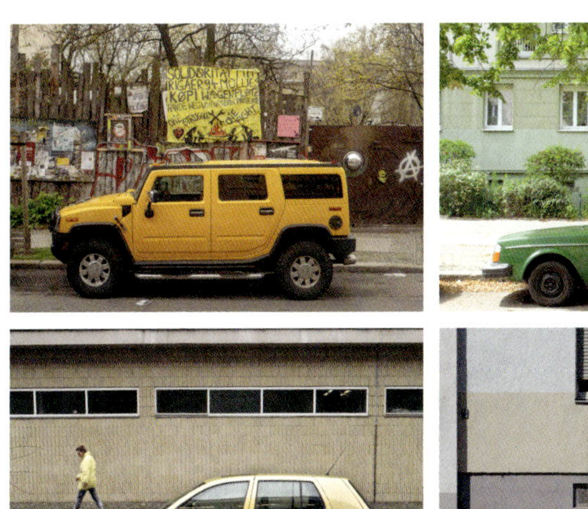

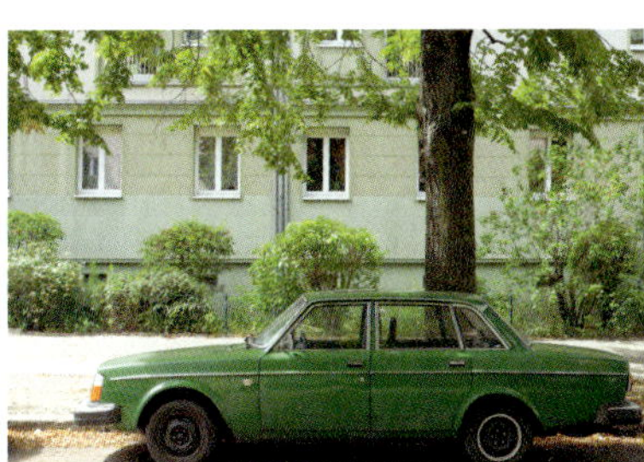

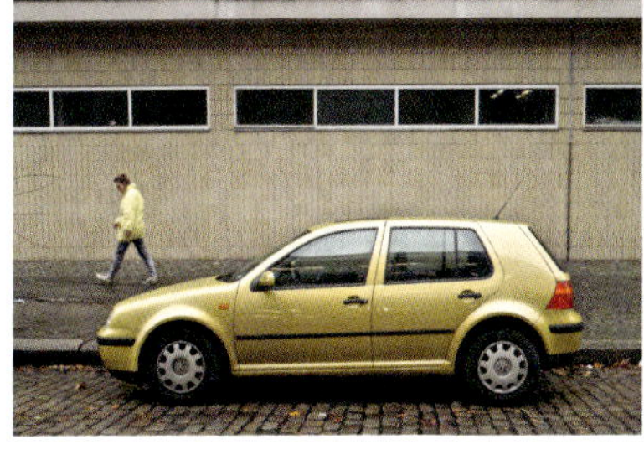

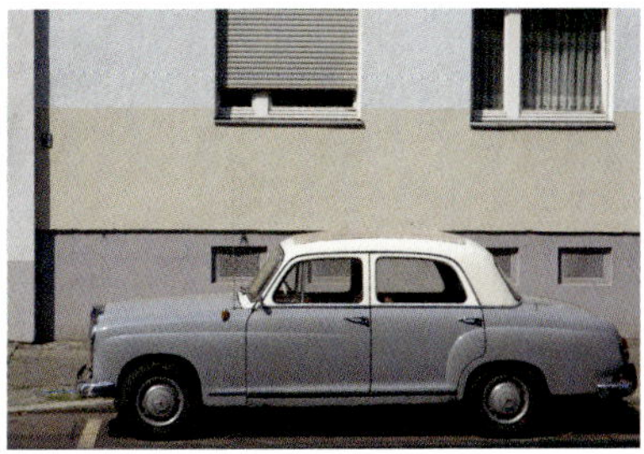

Berlin

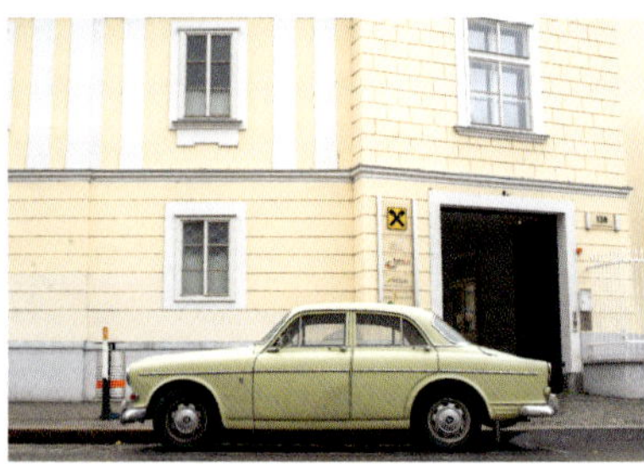
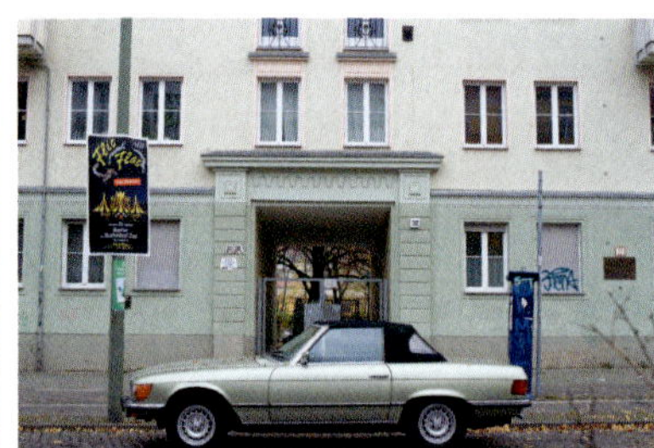
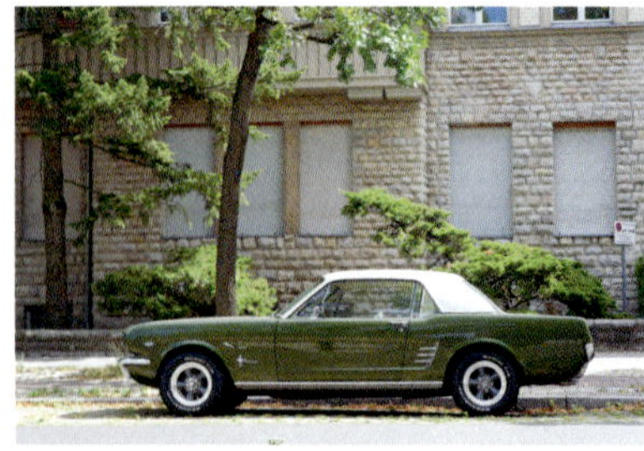
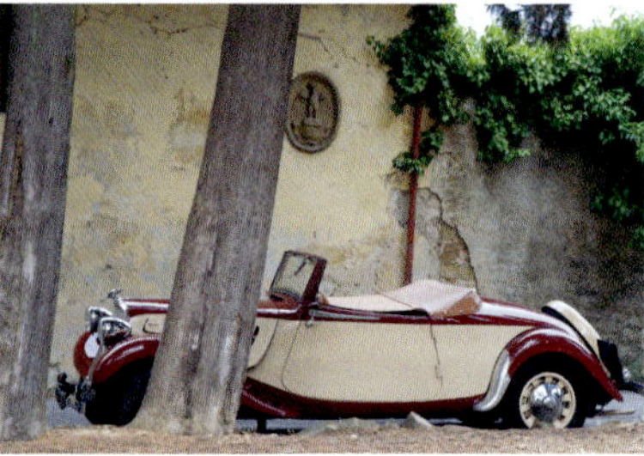

Vienna | Berlin | Florence

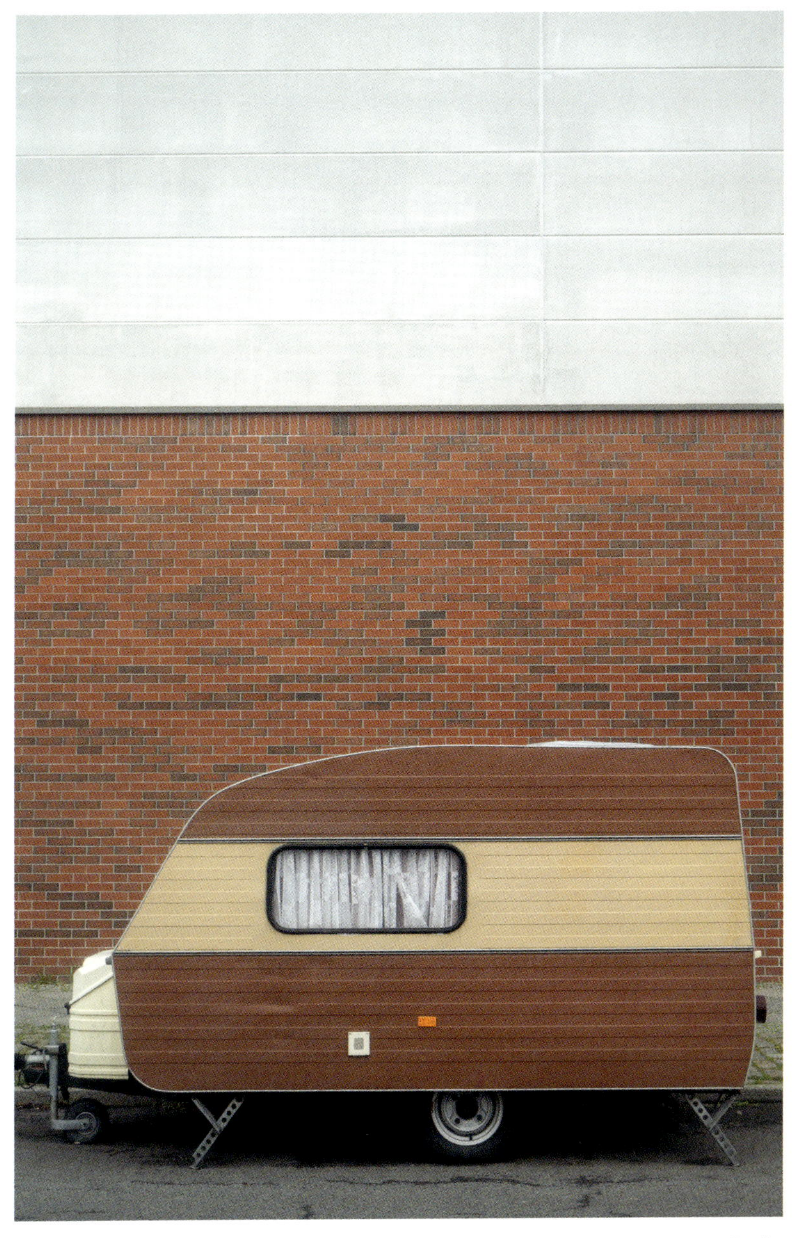

Berlin

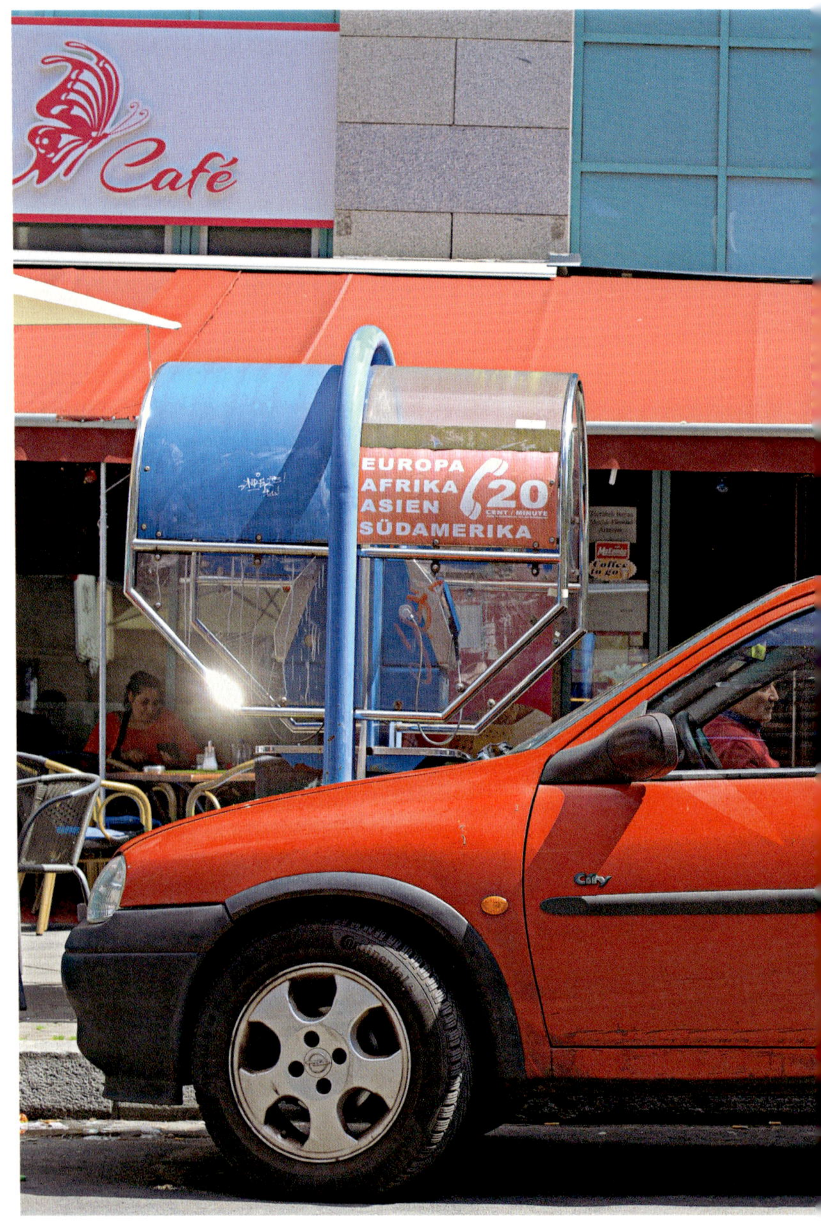
Café
EUROPA
AFRIKA
ASIEN
SÜDAMERIKA
20
CENT / MINUTE

Grüntaler Straße 1
Handyreparatur
ortel
MOBILE
ortel
MOBILE
ORTEL

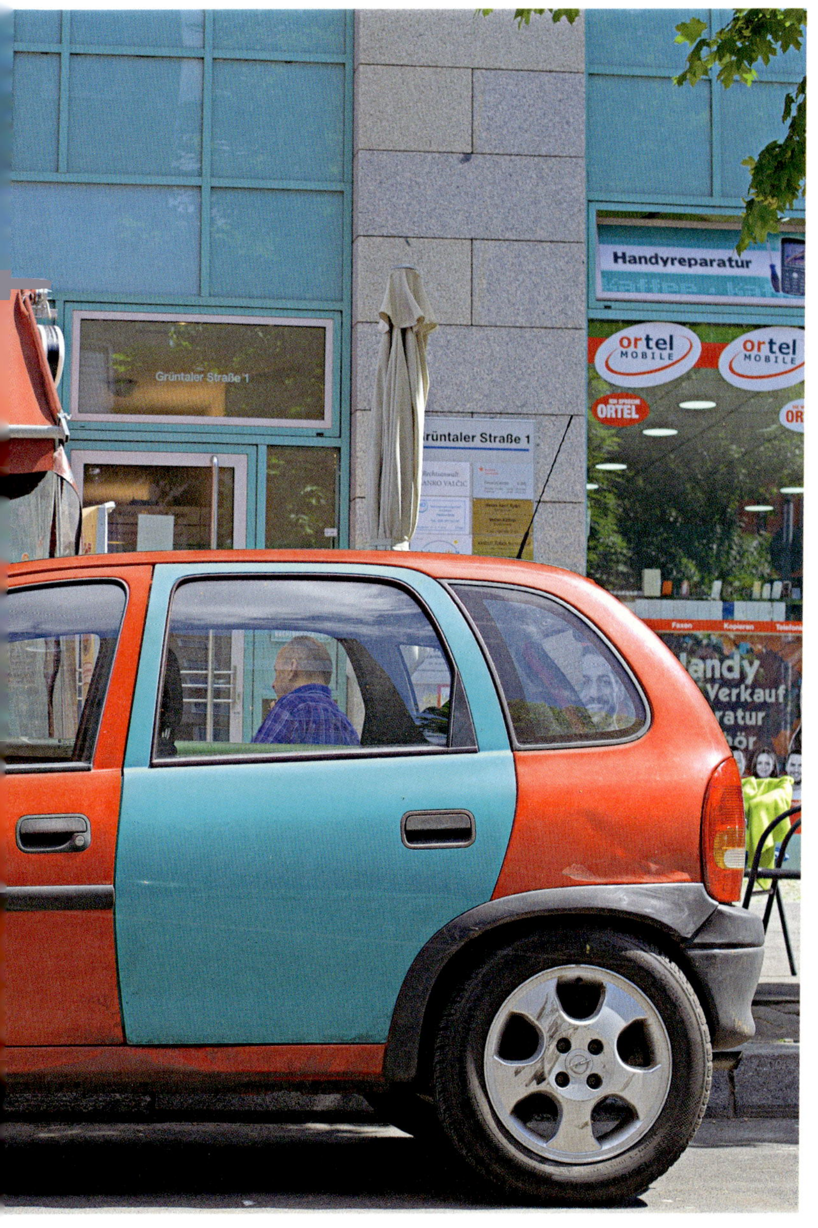

Berlin

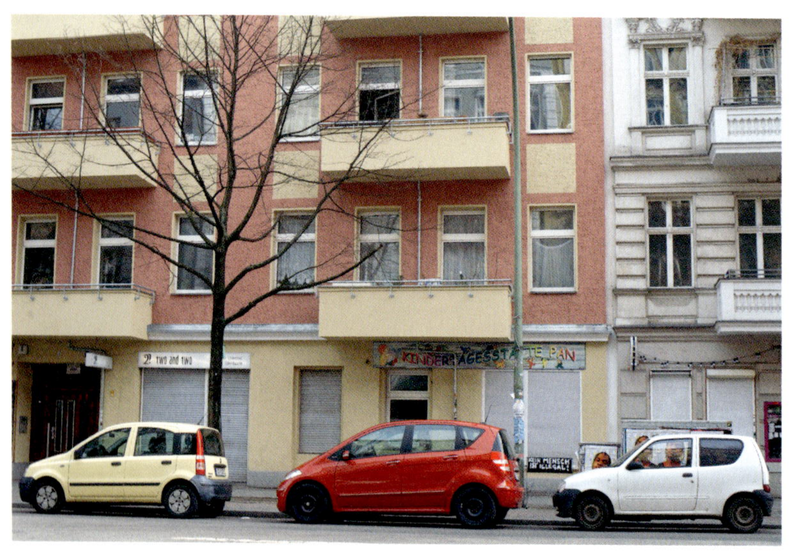

Berlin

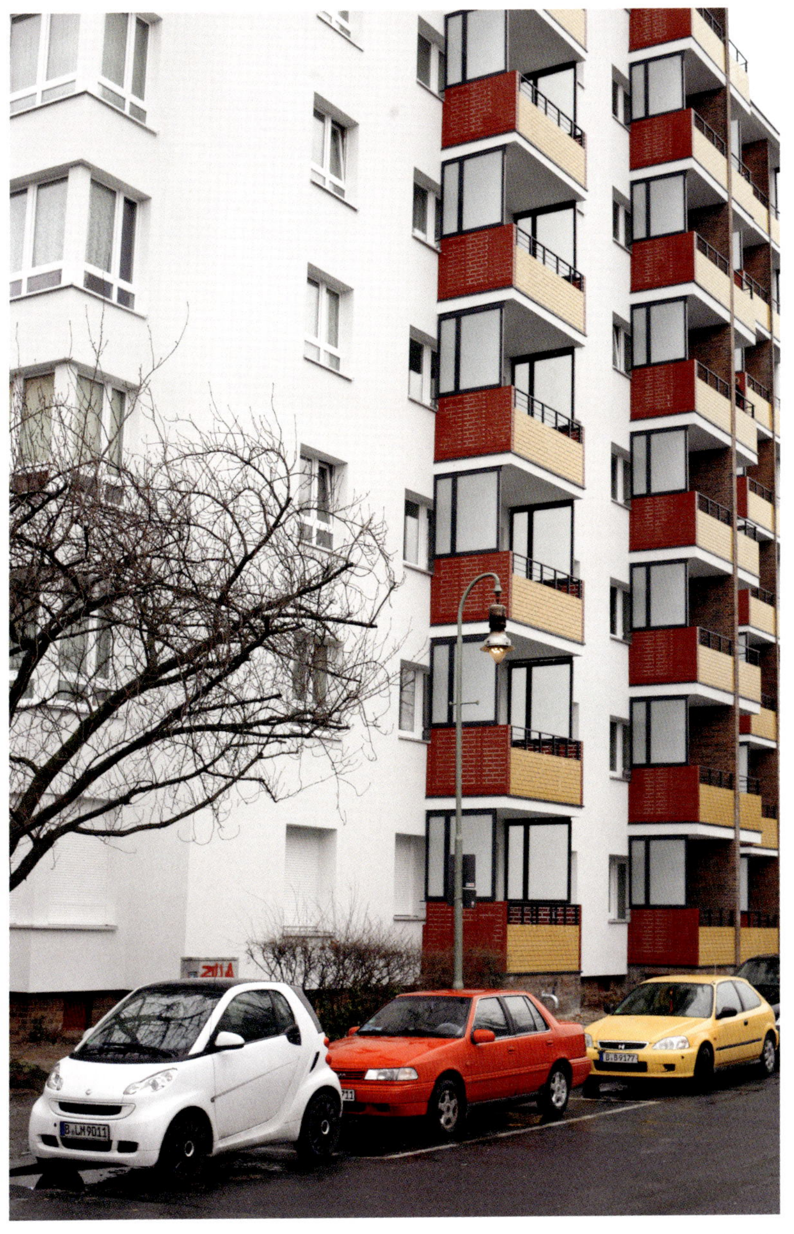

Berlin

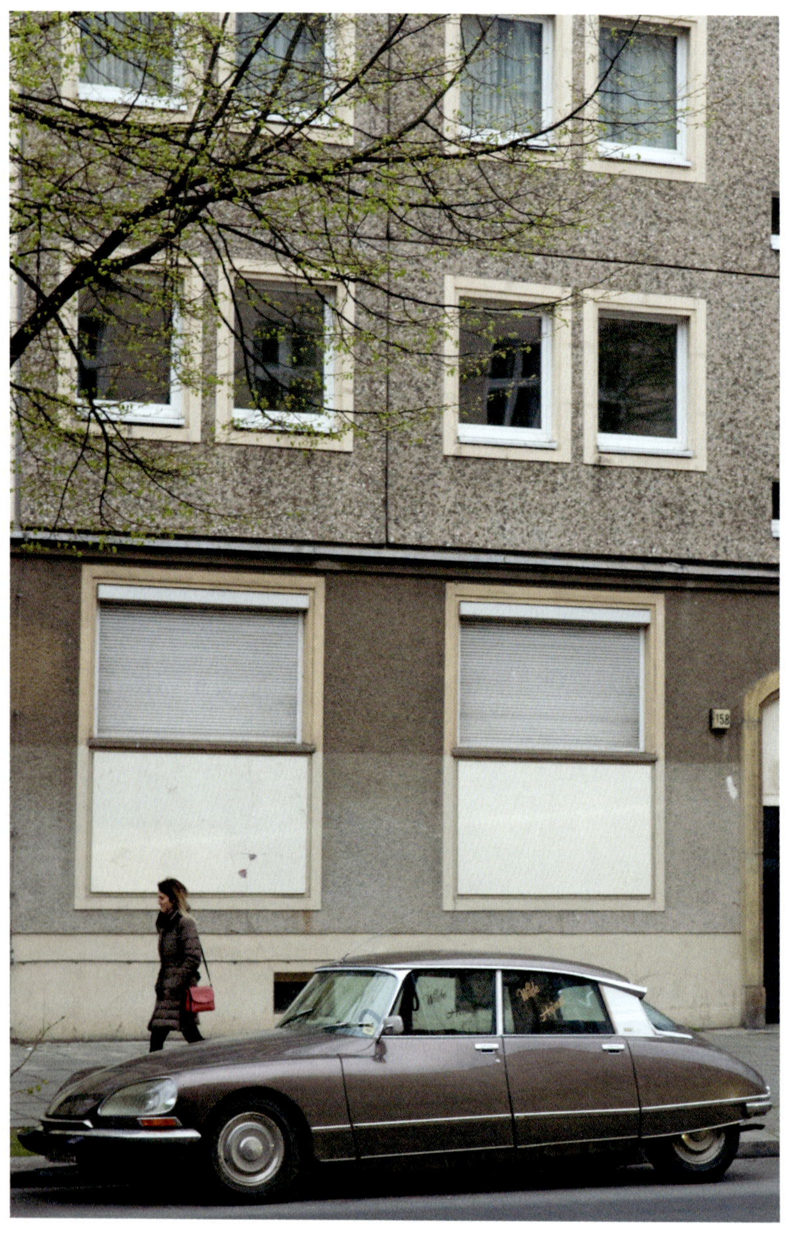

Berlin

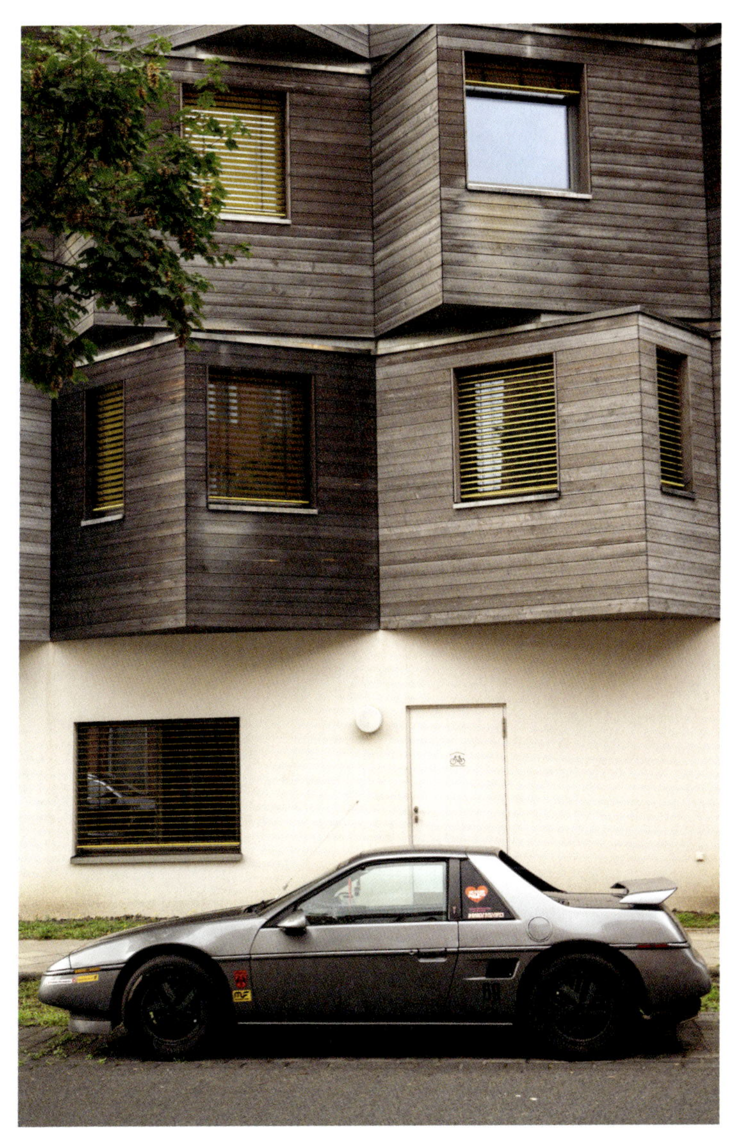

Berlin

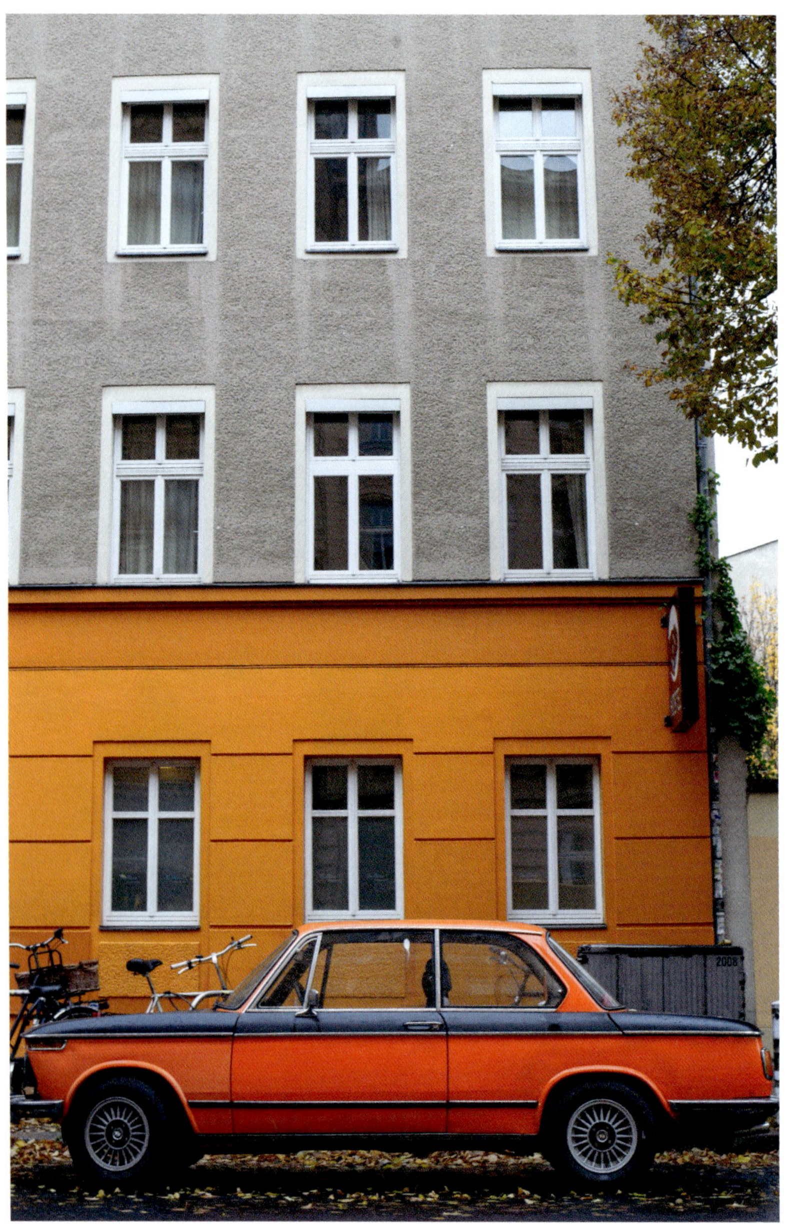

Berlin

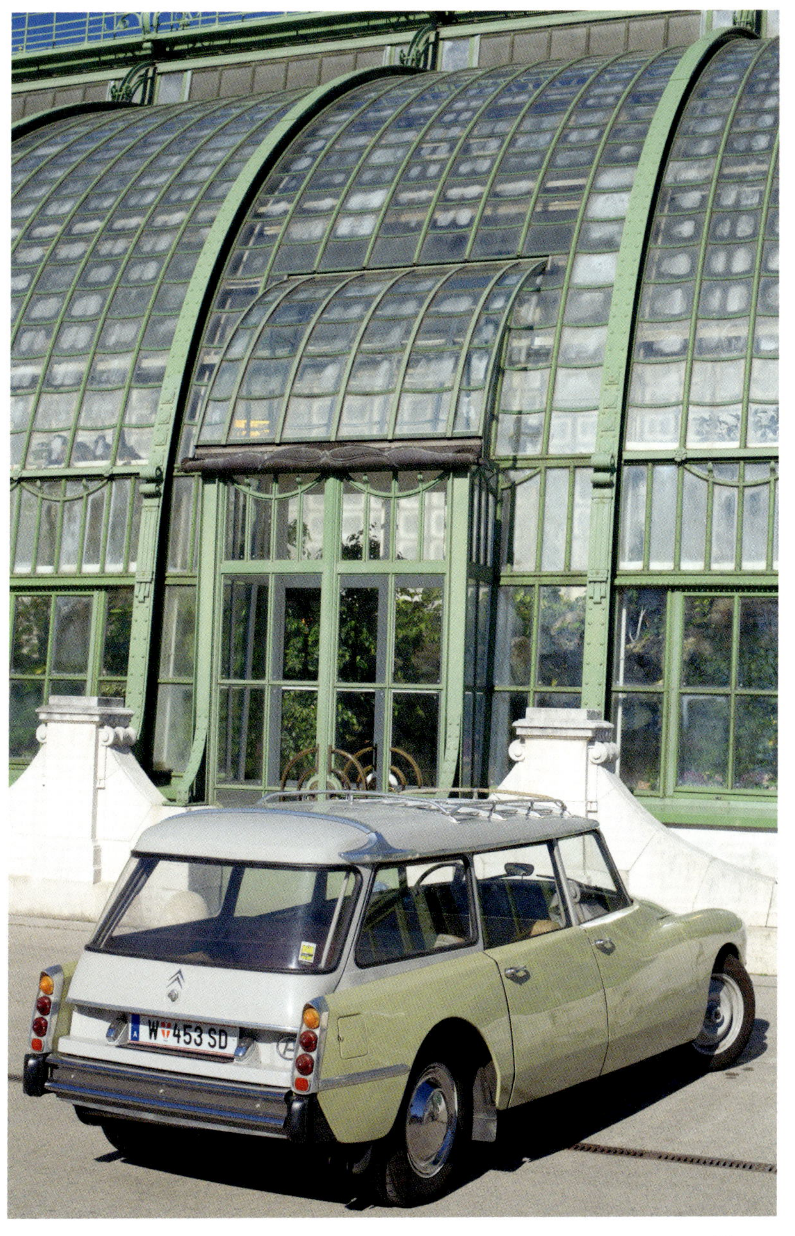

Vienna

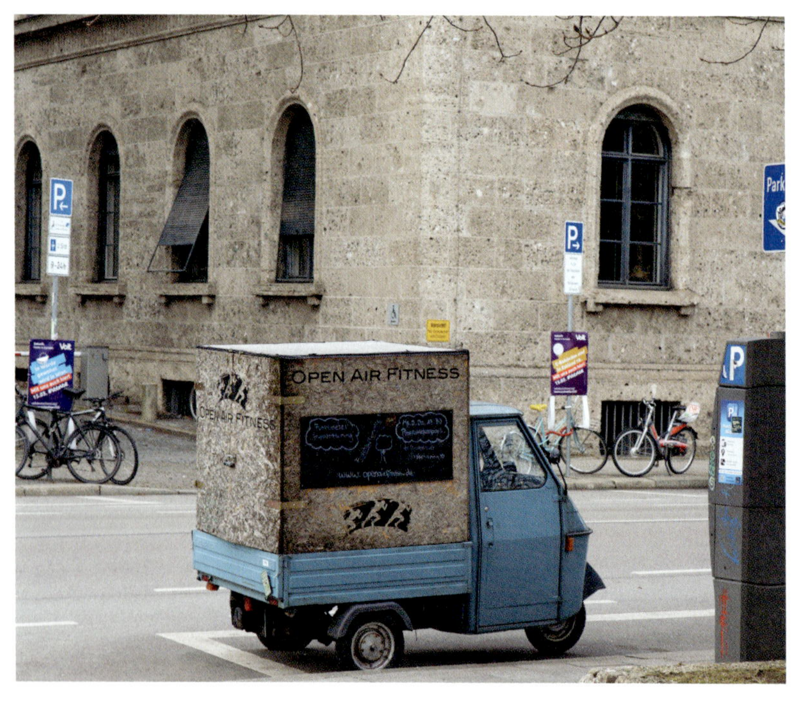

Munich

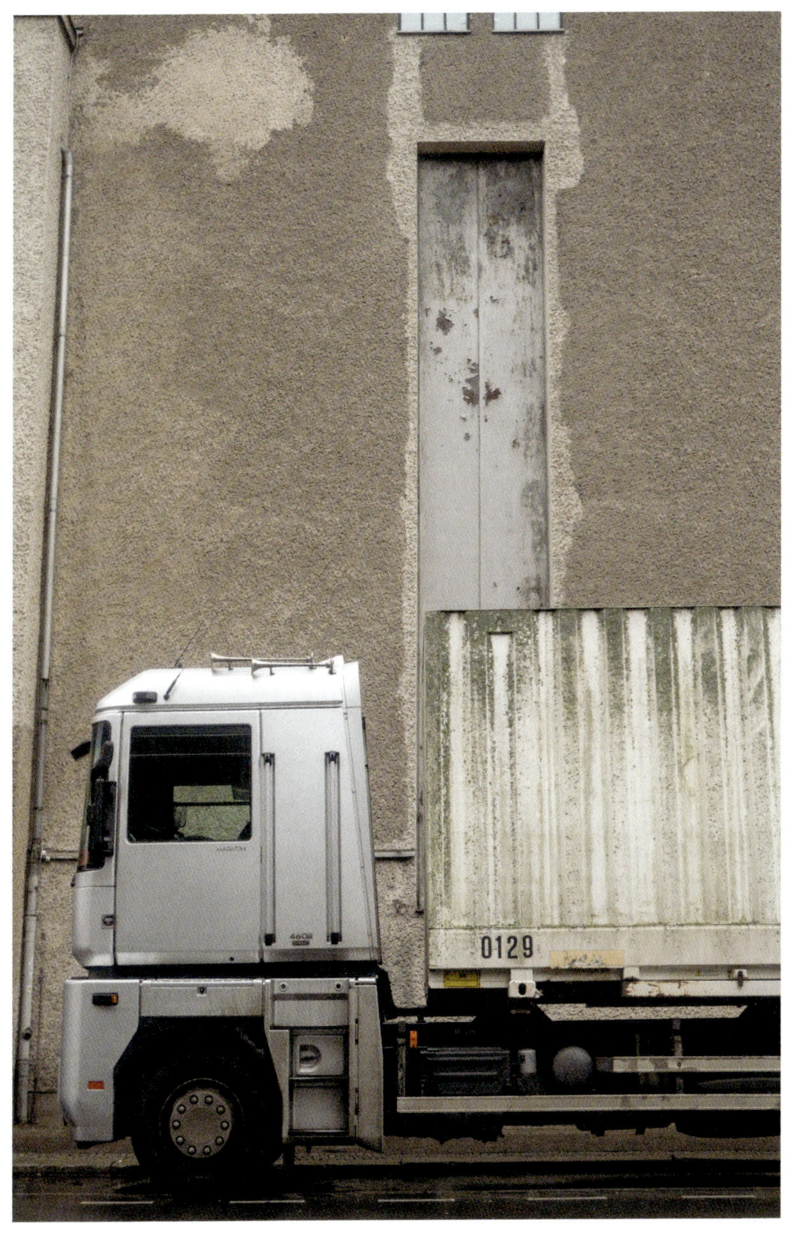

Berlin

MUSE UMS

PEOPLE MATCHING ARTWORKS 2017–2024

Is it pure coincidence when people position themselves in front of a particular work of art, when they feel attracted to a certain art object? Perhaps it is the elective affinities that lead to the perfect matches, the correspondences between picture and viewer that Stefan Draschan captures after patiently waiting for the decisive moment.

Ist es reiner Zufall, wer sich vor welchem Kunstwerk positioniert, wer sich von welchem Kunstobjekt angezogen fühlt? Vielleicht sind es auch Wahlverwandtschaften, die zu den „perfect matches", den Übereinstimmungen zwischen Bild und Betrachtenden führen, die Stefan Draschan nach geduldigem Abwarten im entscheidenden Moment festhält.

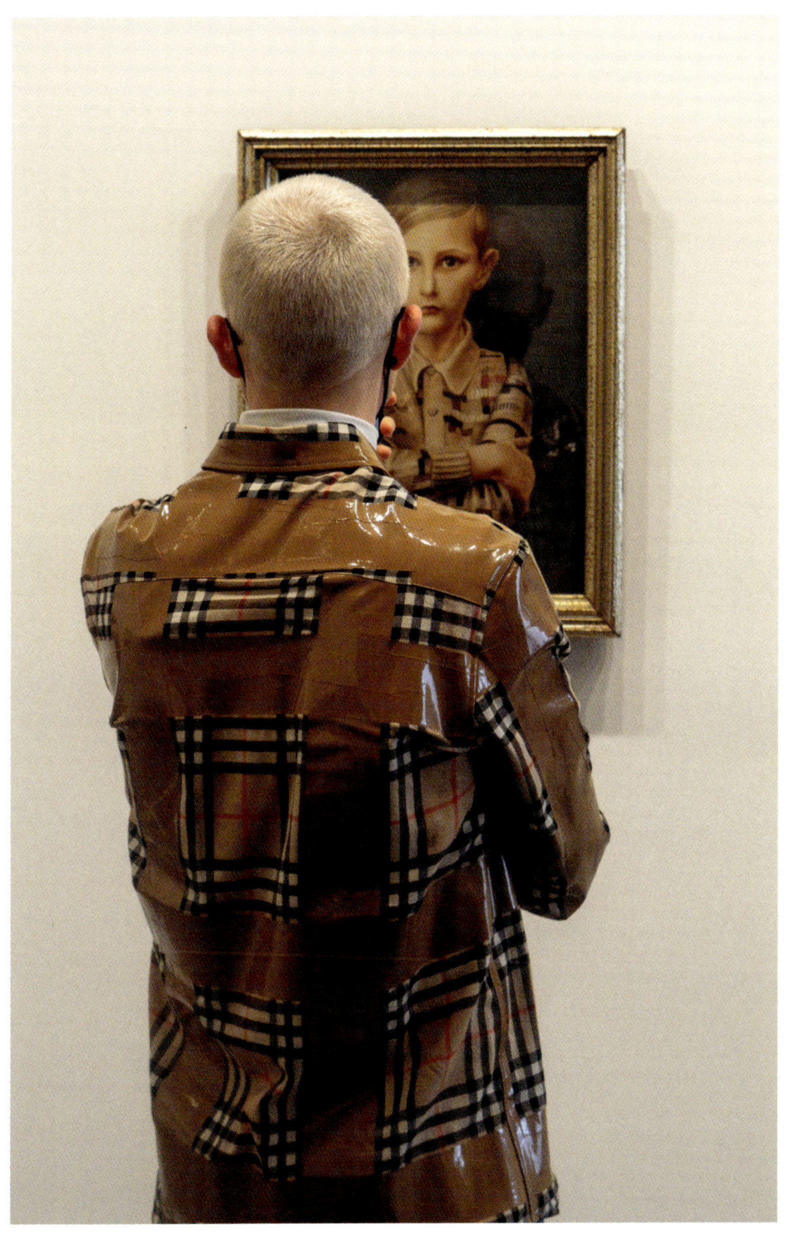

Günther, Neue Nationalgalerie, Berlin

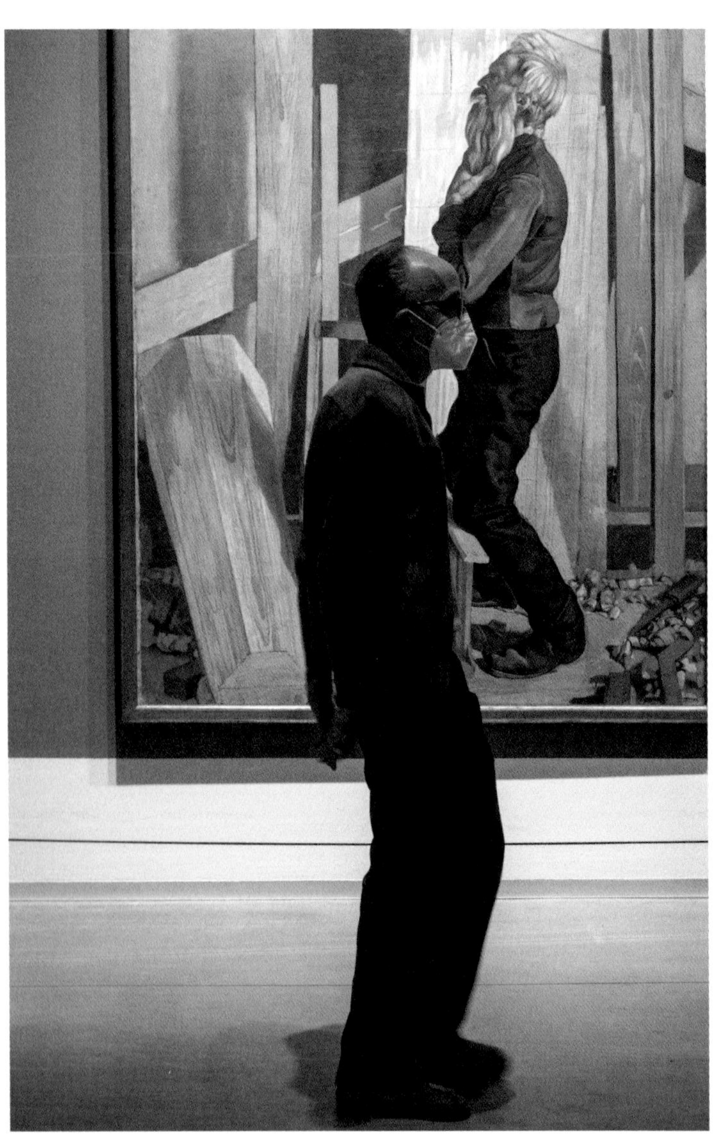

Hodler, Berlinische Galerie, Berlin

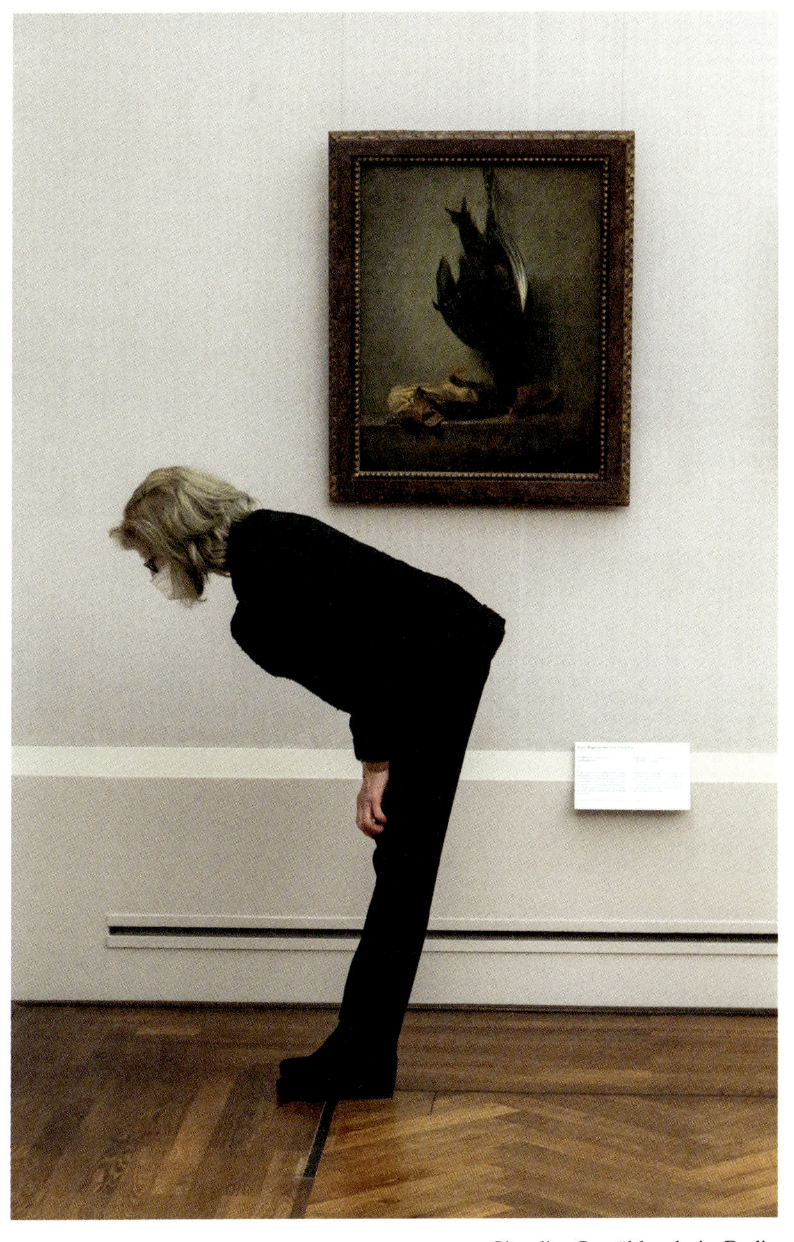

Chardin, Gemäldegalerie, Berlin

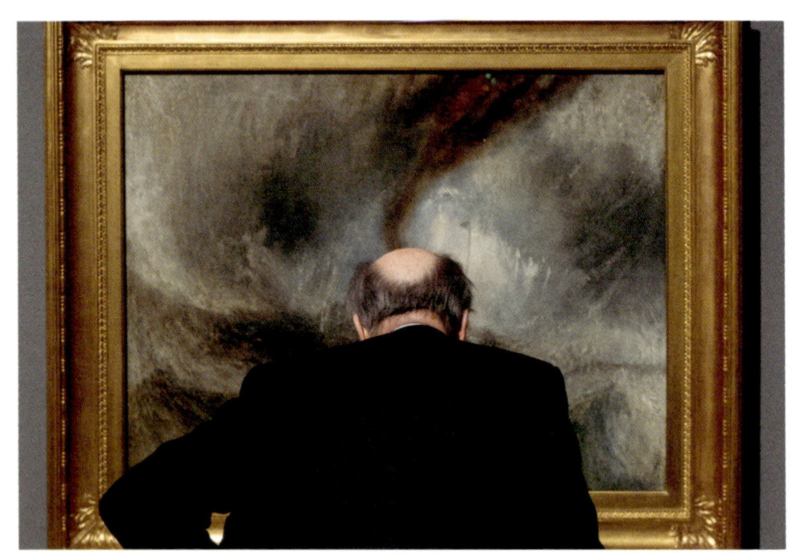

Turner, Lenbachhaus, Munich

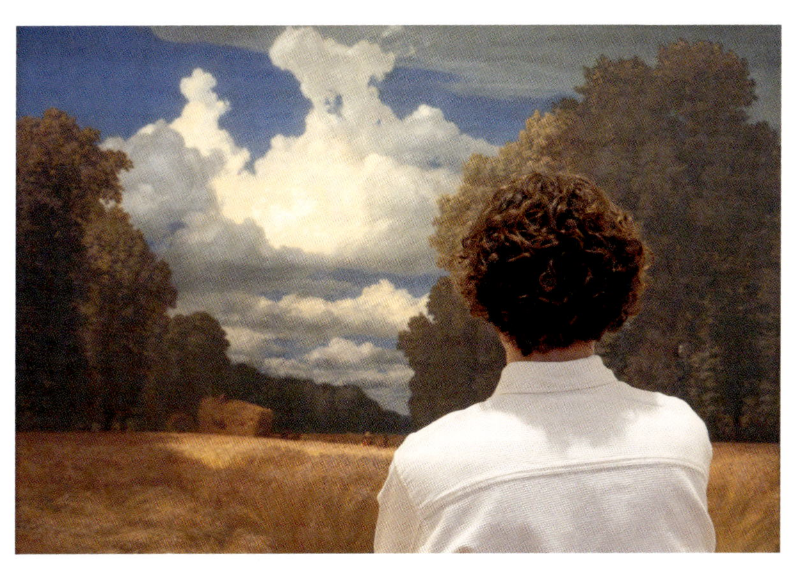

Zünd, Kunstmuseum Basel

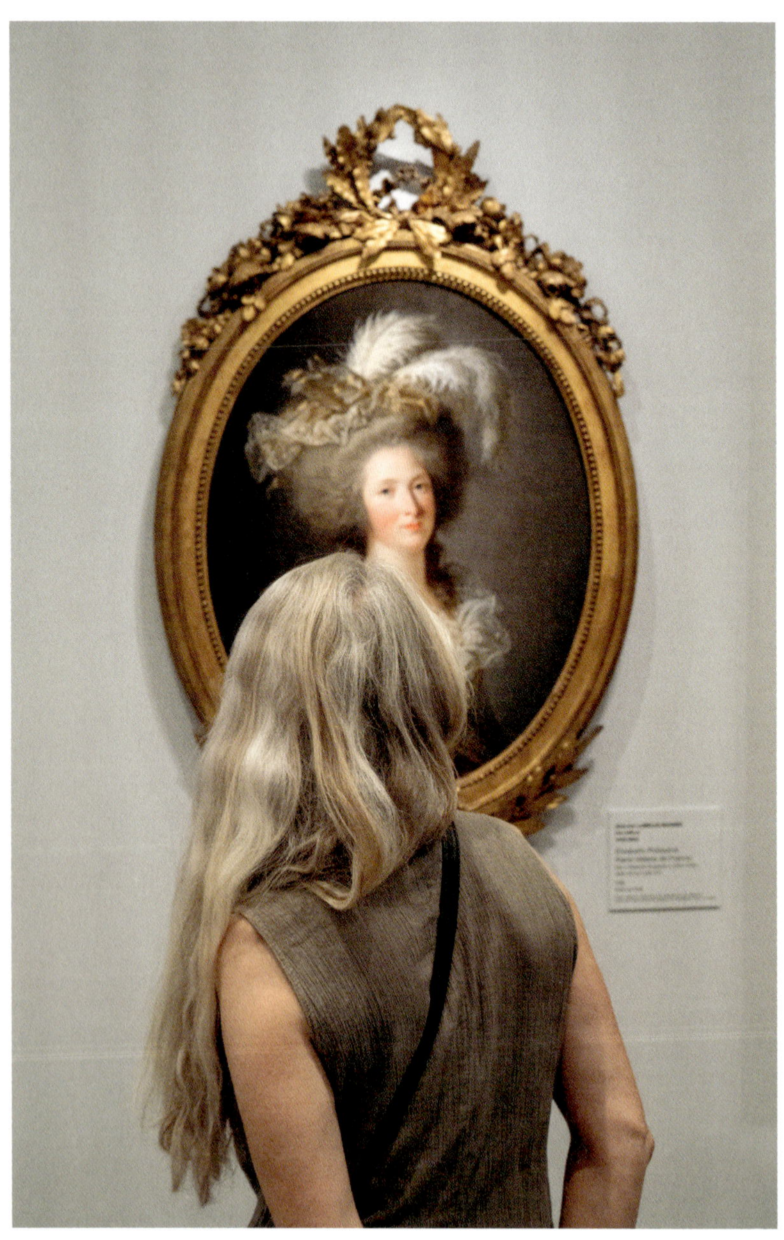

Labille-Guiard, Musée du Luxembourg, Paris

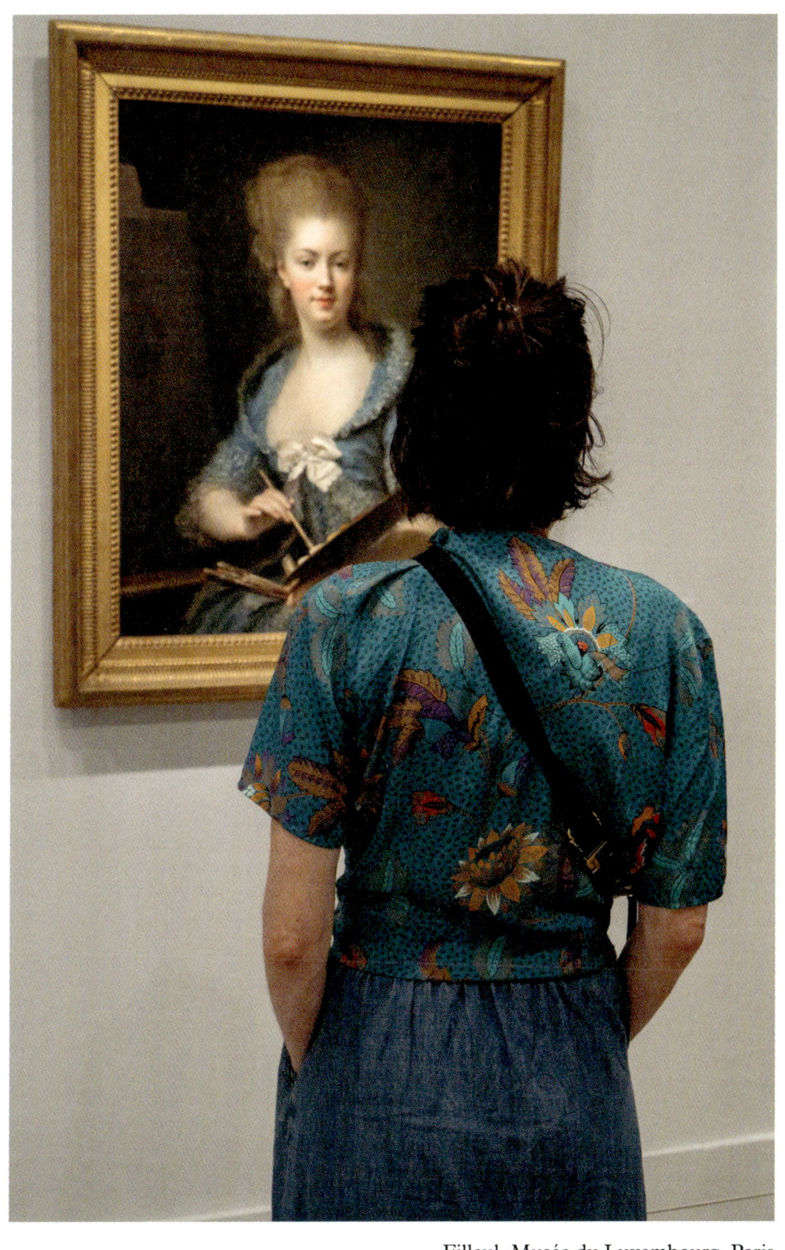

Filleul, Musée du Luxembourg, Paris

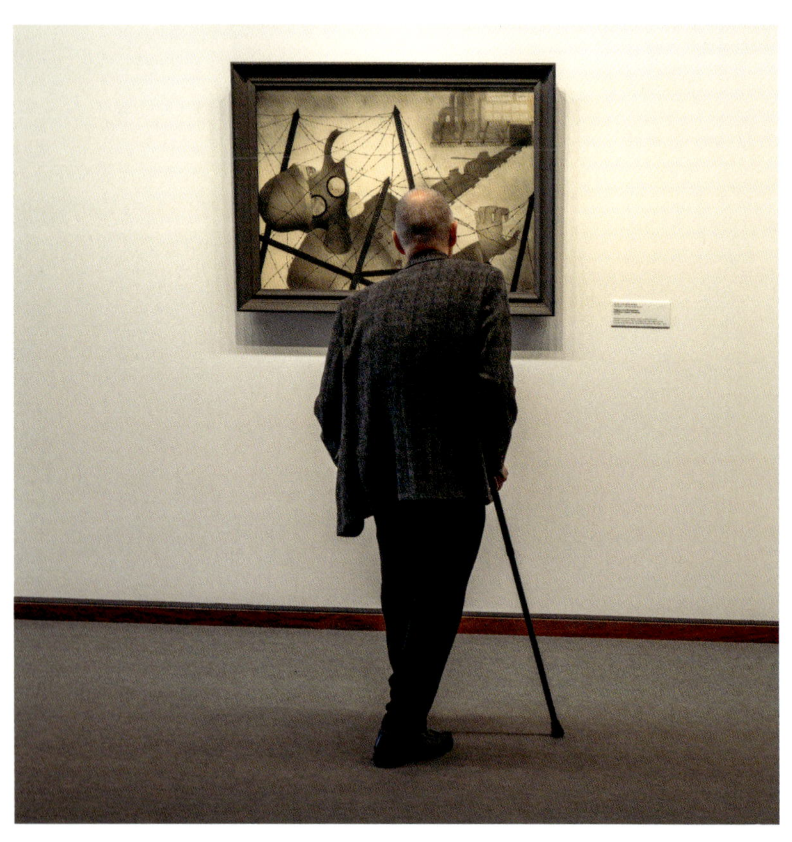

Lex-Nerlinger, Neue Nationalgalerie, Berlin

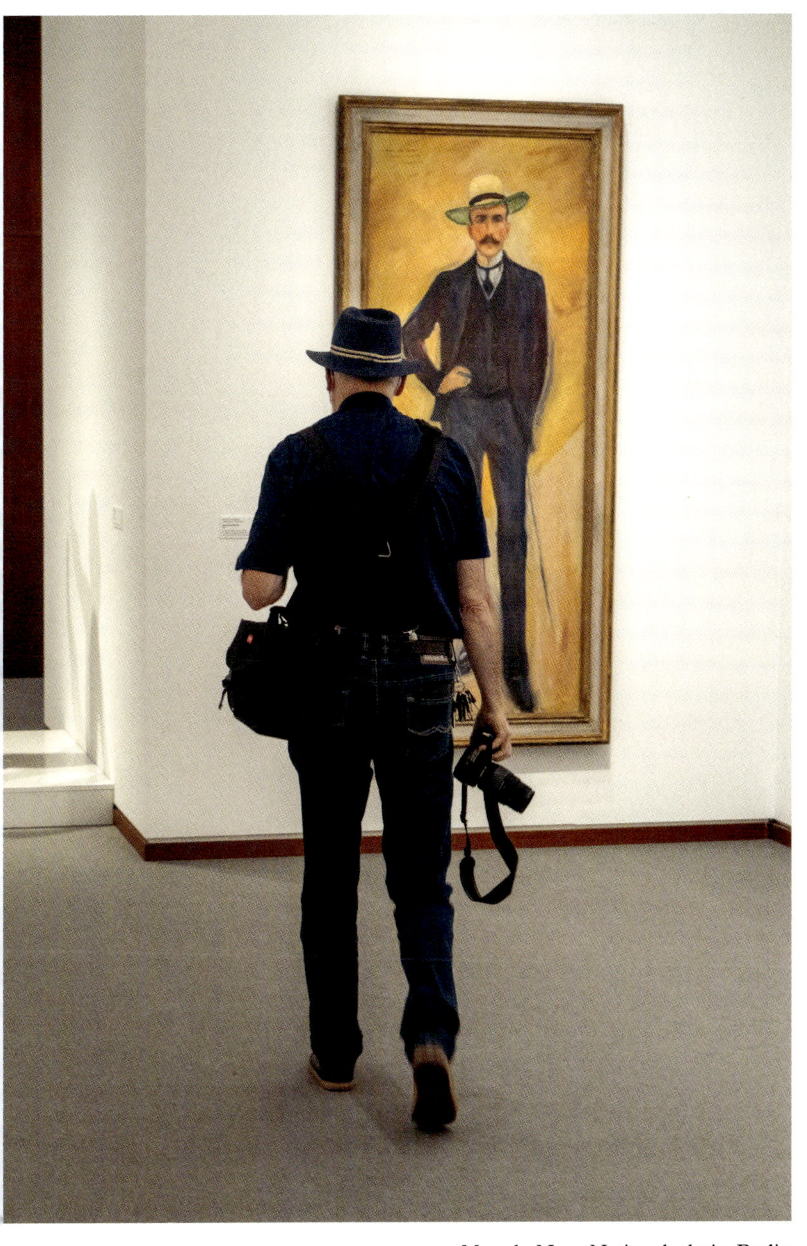

Munch, Neue Nationalgalerie, Berlin

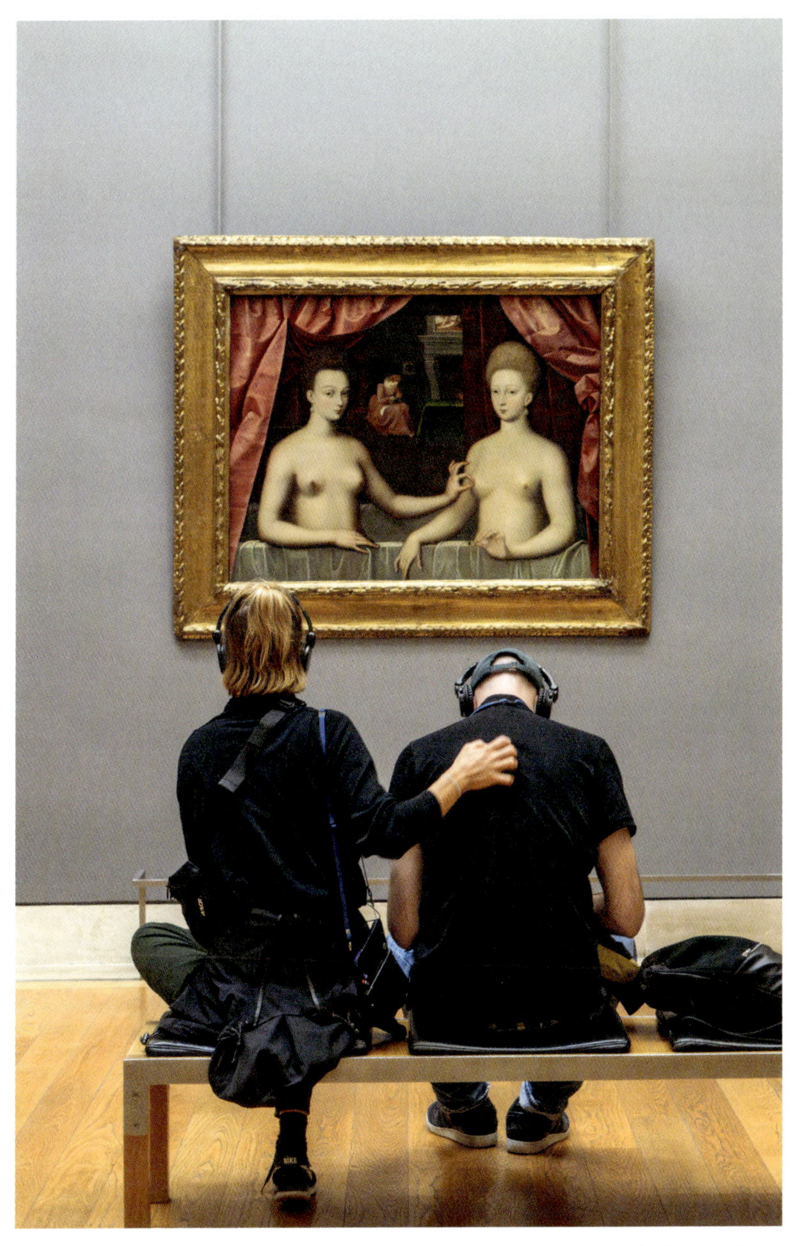

School of Fontainebleau, Musée du Louvre, Paris

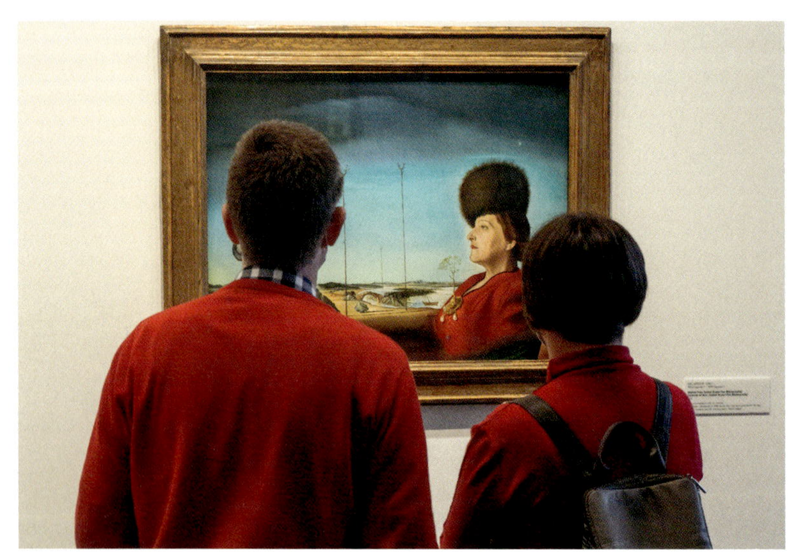

Dalí, Neue Nationalgalerie, Berlin

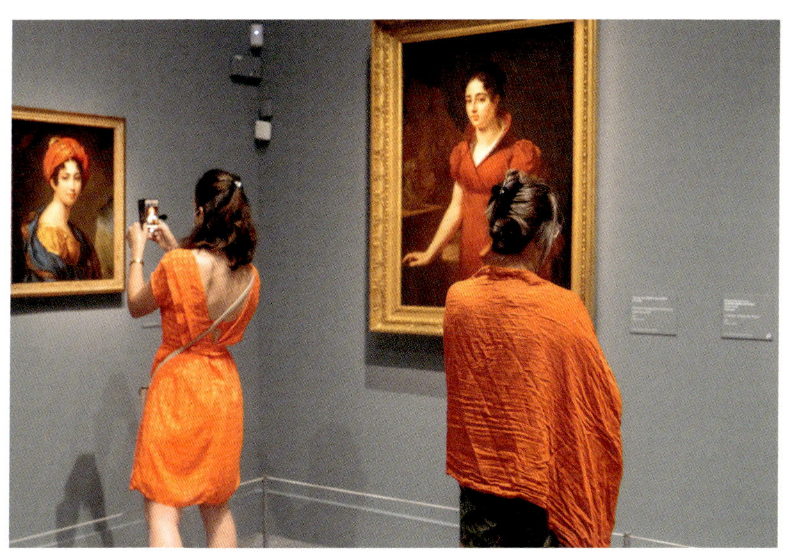

Jeangros & Duvidal de Montferrier, Musée du Luxembourg, Paris

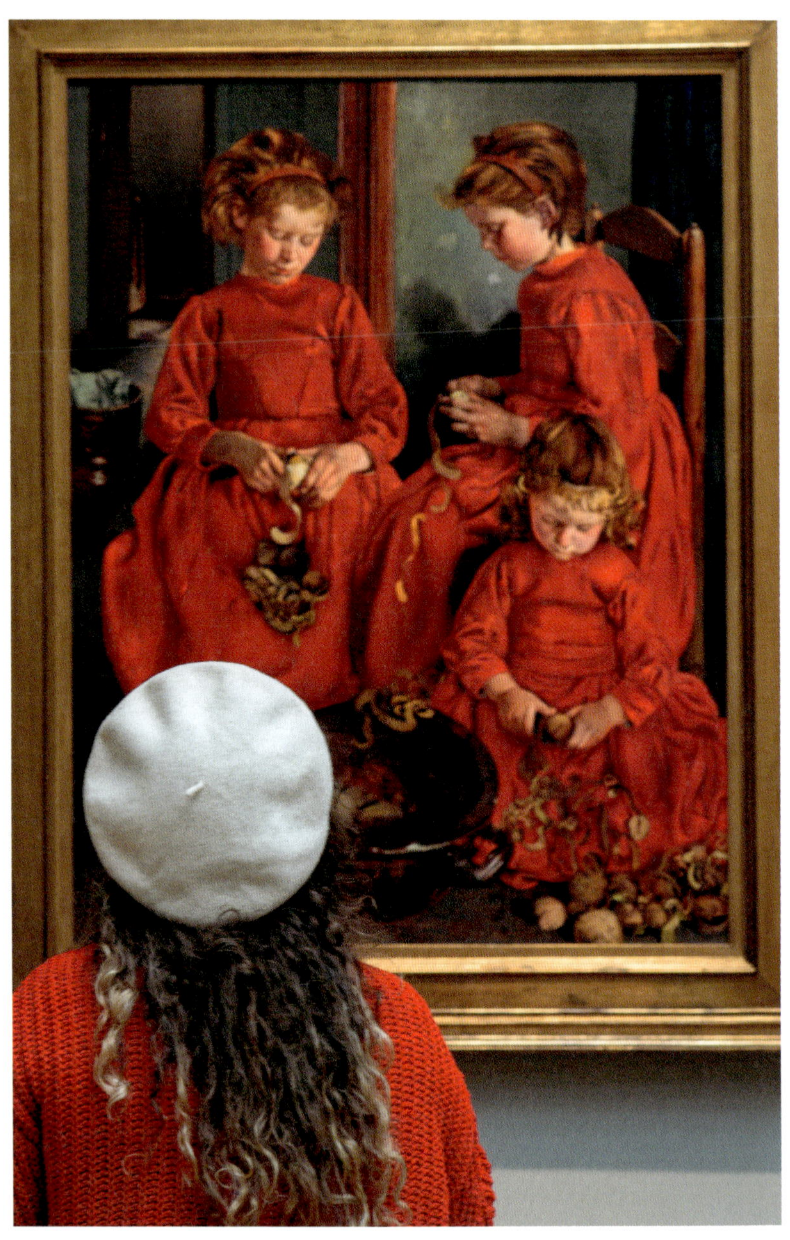

Frédéric, The Metropolitan Museum of Art, New York

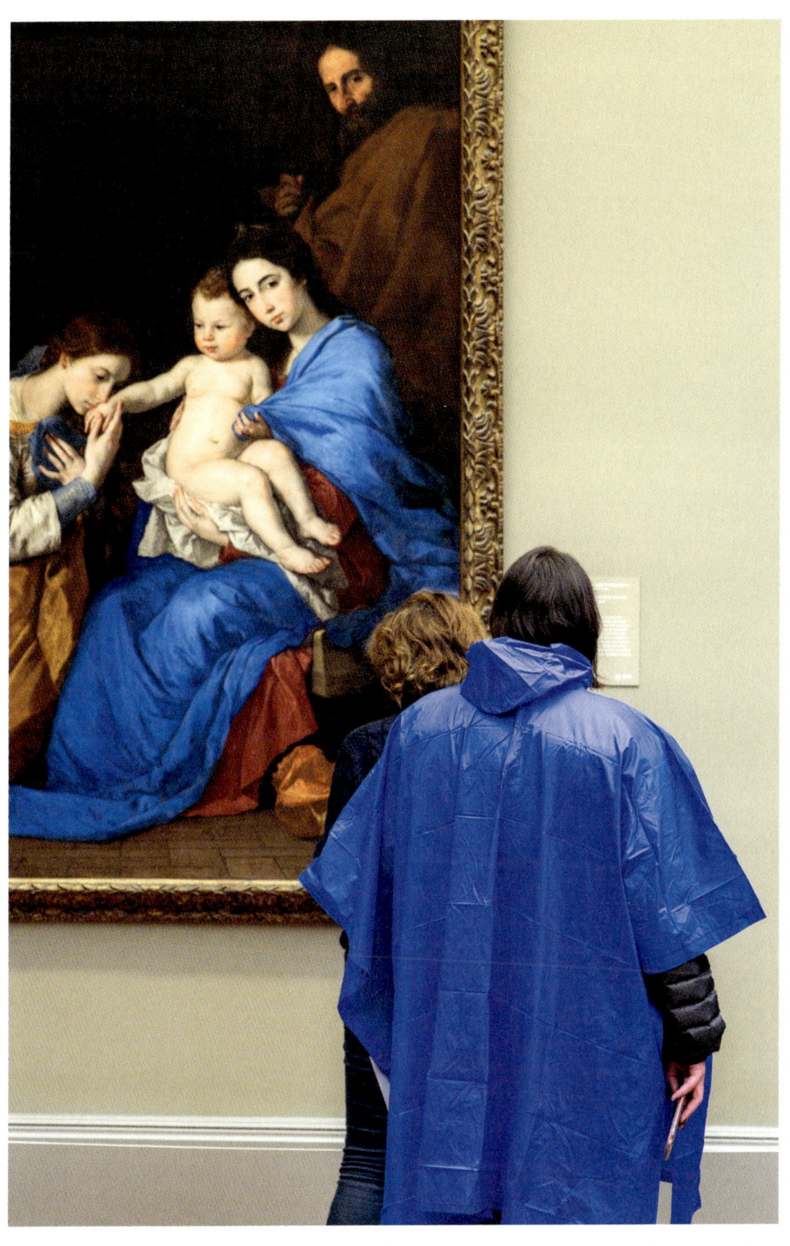

de Ribera, The Metropolitan Museum of Art, New York

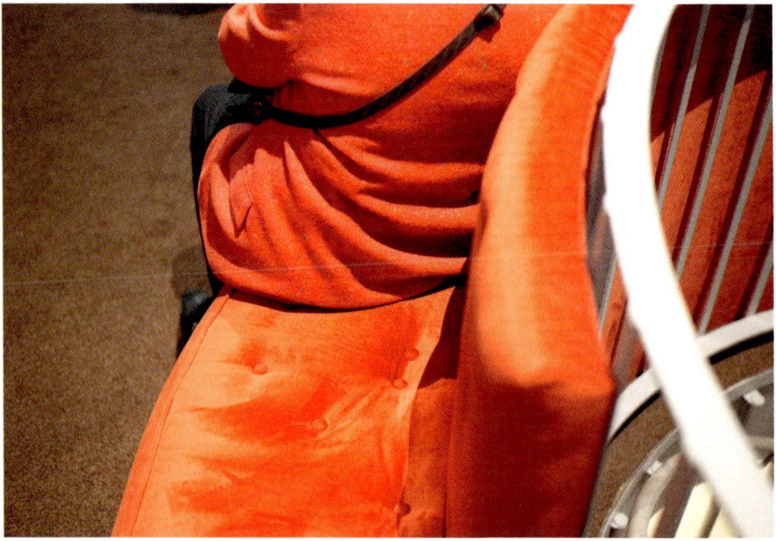

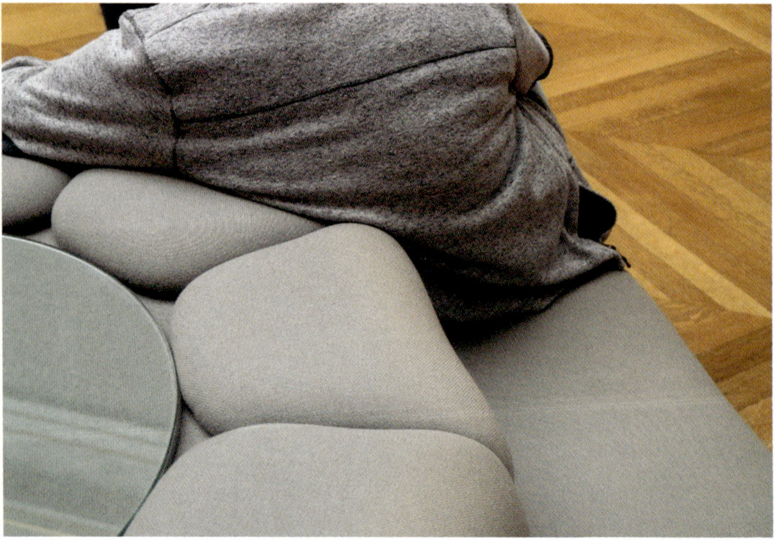

Musée de la Vie Romantique, Paris | Musée du Louvre, Paris

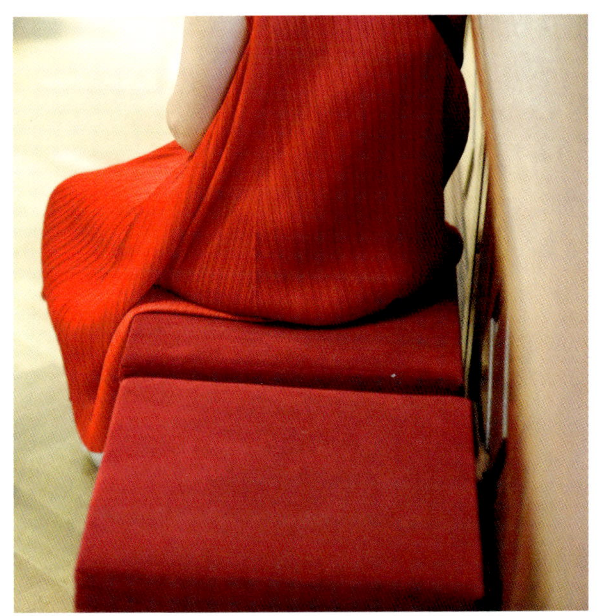

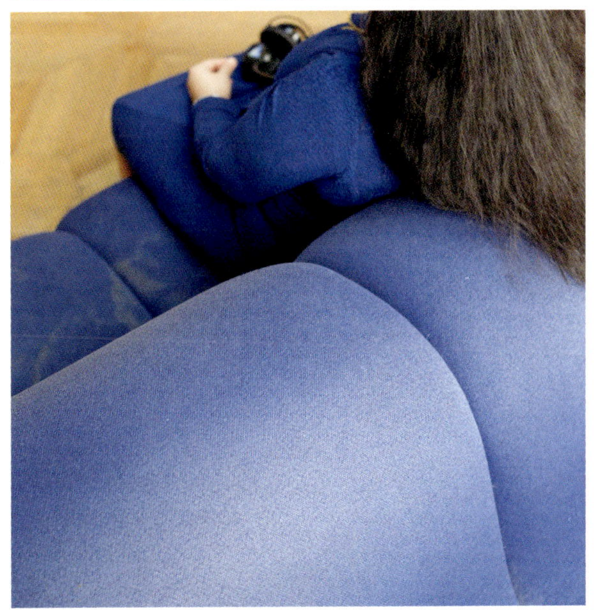

Kunsthistorisches Museum, Vienna | Musée du Louvre, Paris

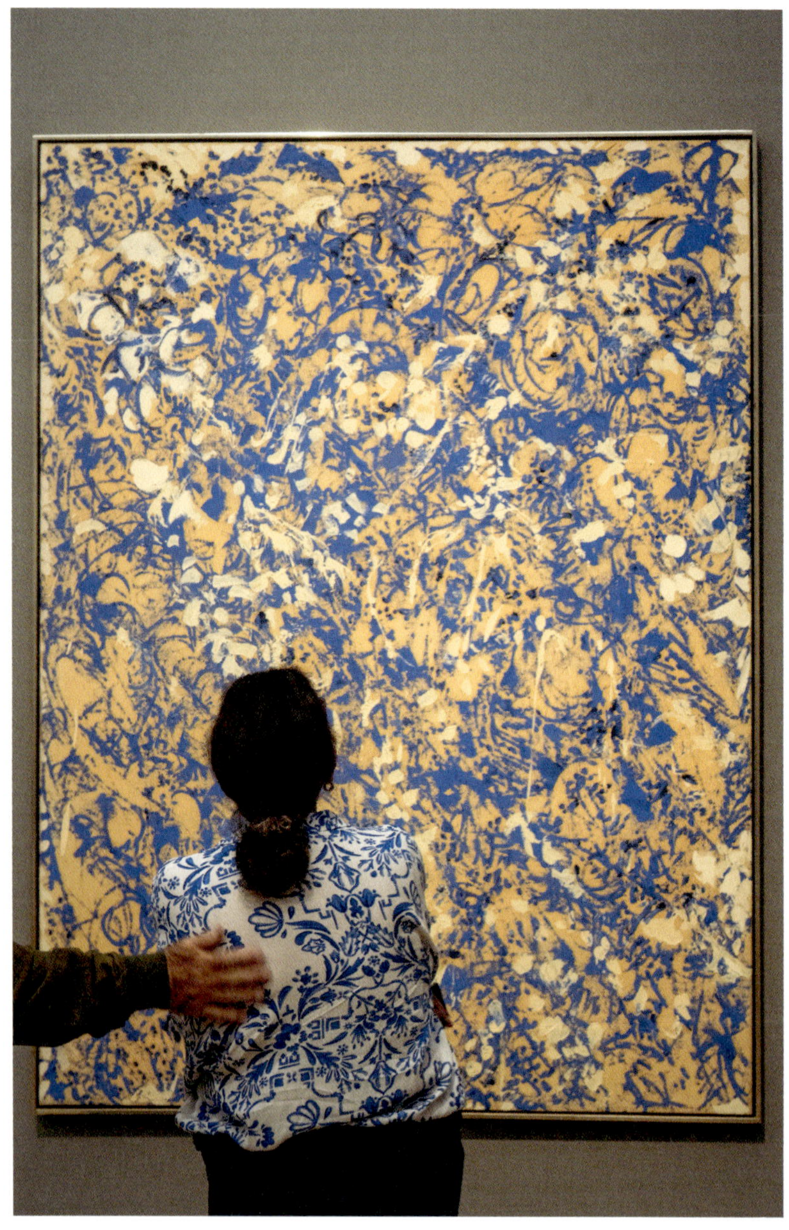

Krasner, Museum Barberini, Potsdam

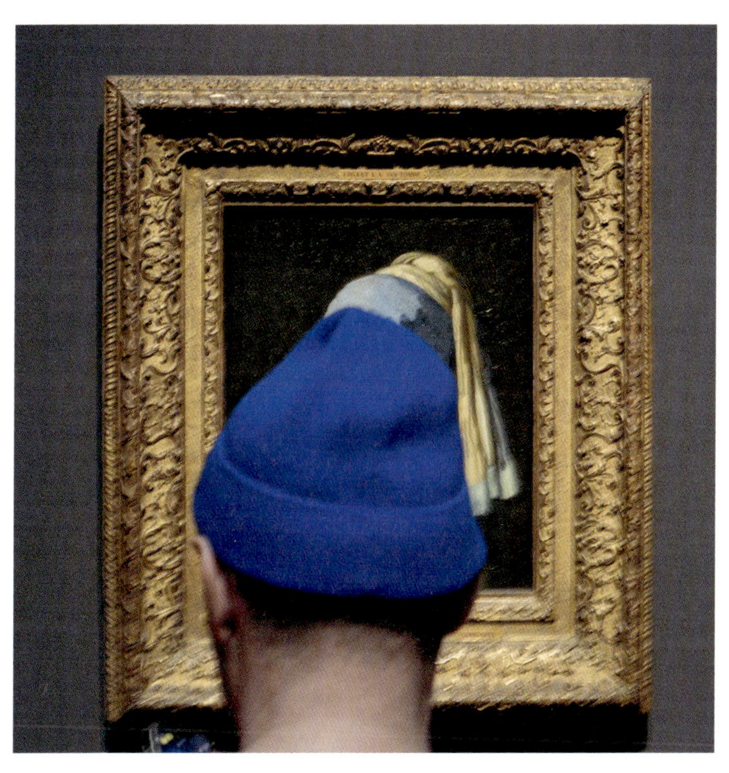

Vermeer, Rijksmuseum, Amsterdam

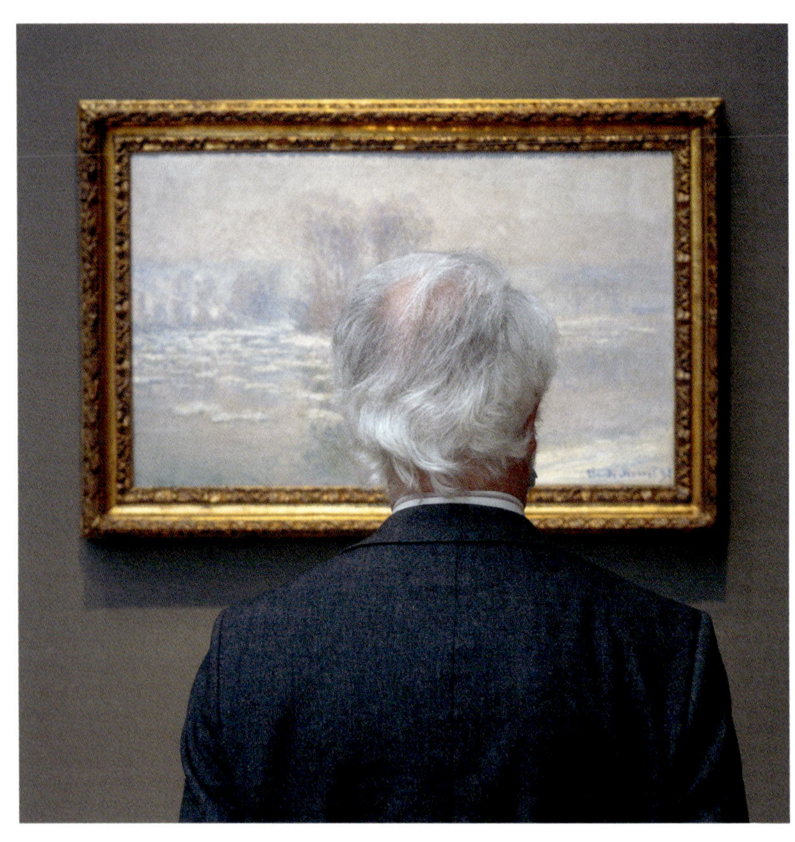

Monet, Museum Barberini, Potsdam

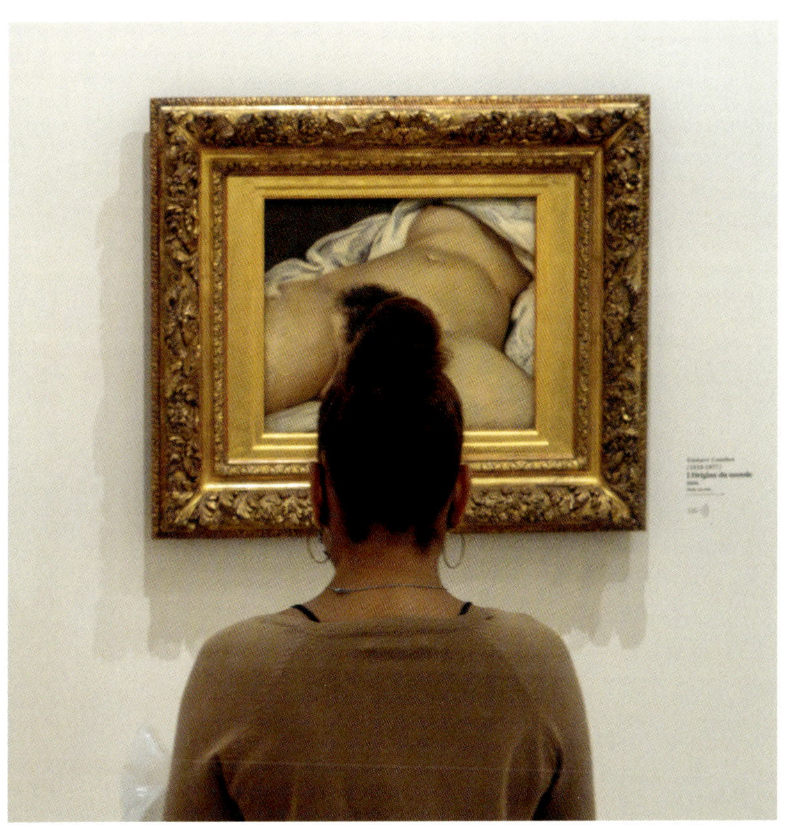

Courbet, Musée d'Orsay, Paris

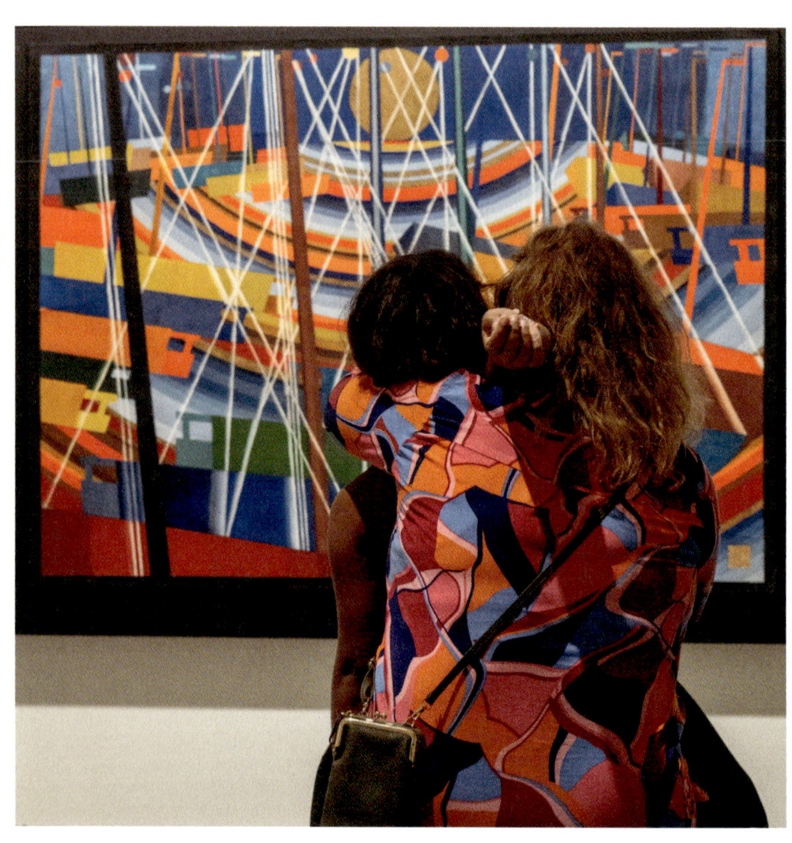

Wiederhold, Neue Nationalgalerie, Berlin

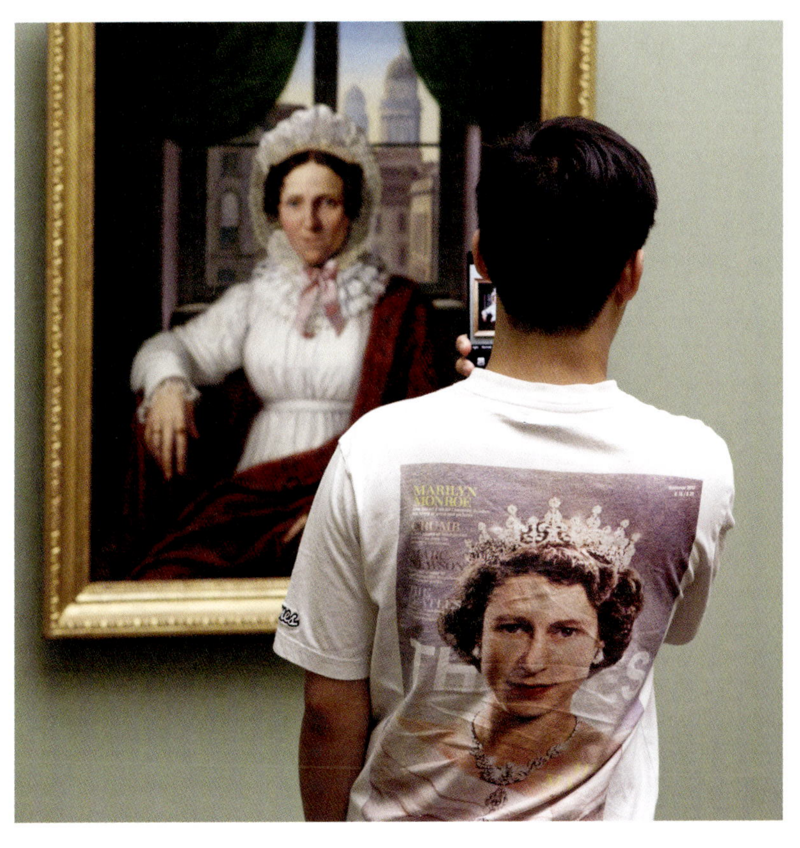

Hummel, Alte Nationalgalerie, Berlin

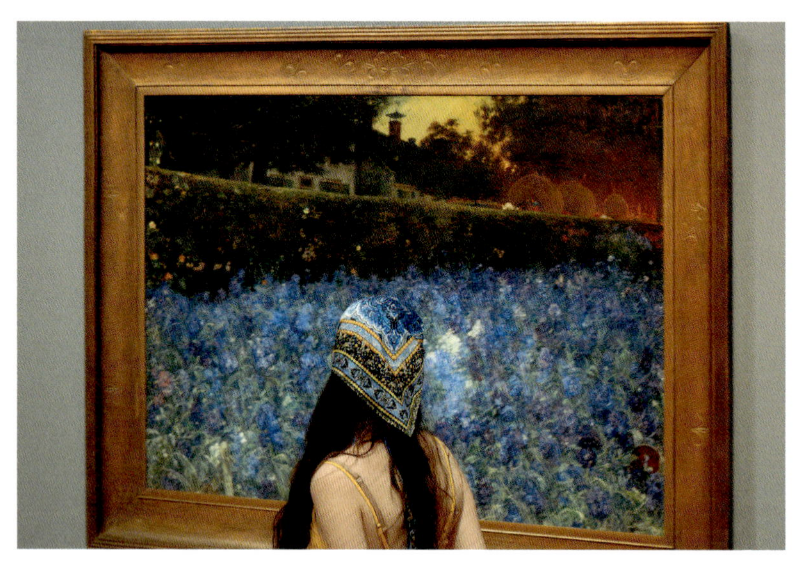

Van Looy, Museum Barberini, Potsdam

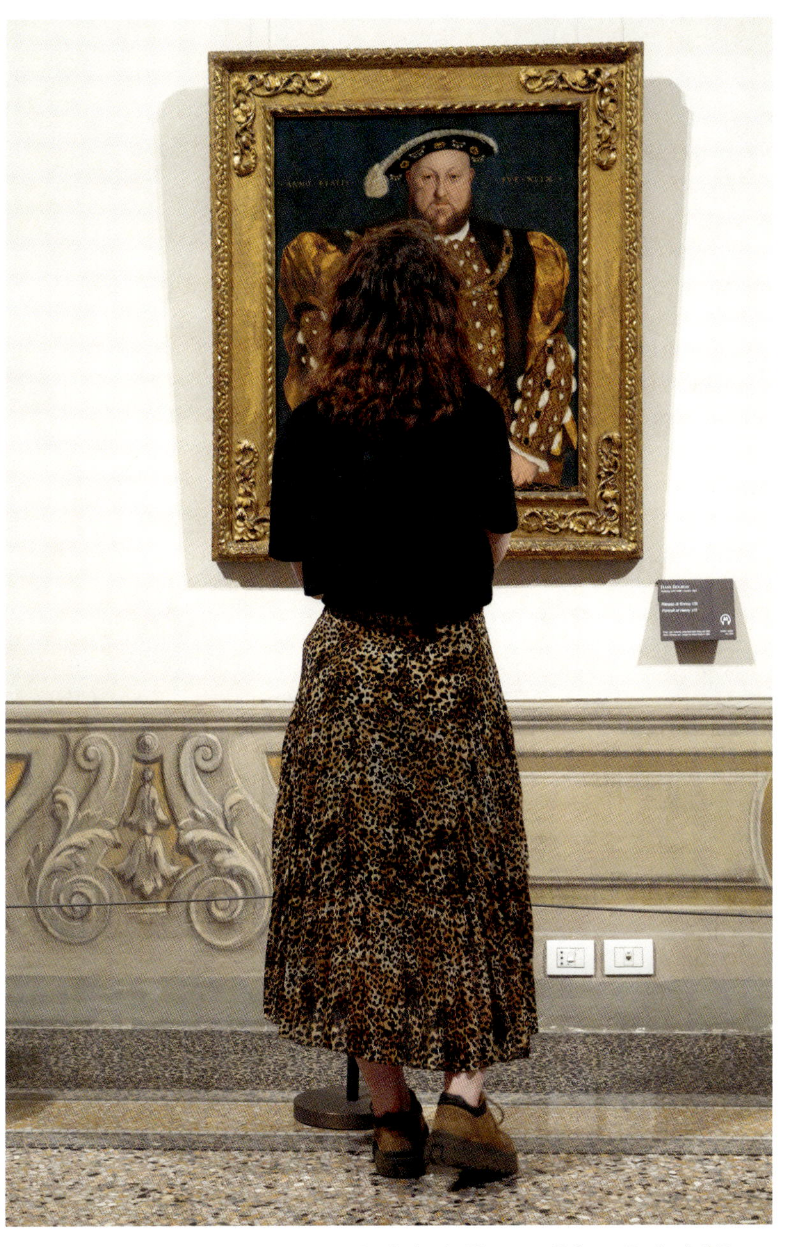

Holbein the Younger, Palazzo Barberini, Rome

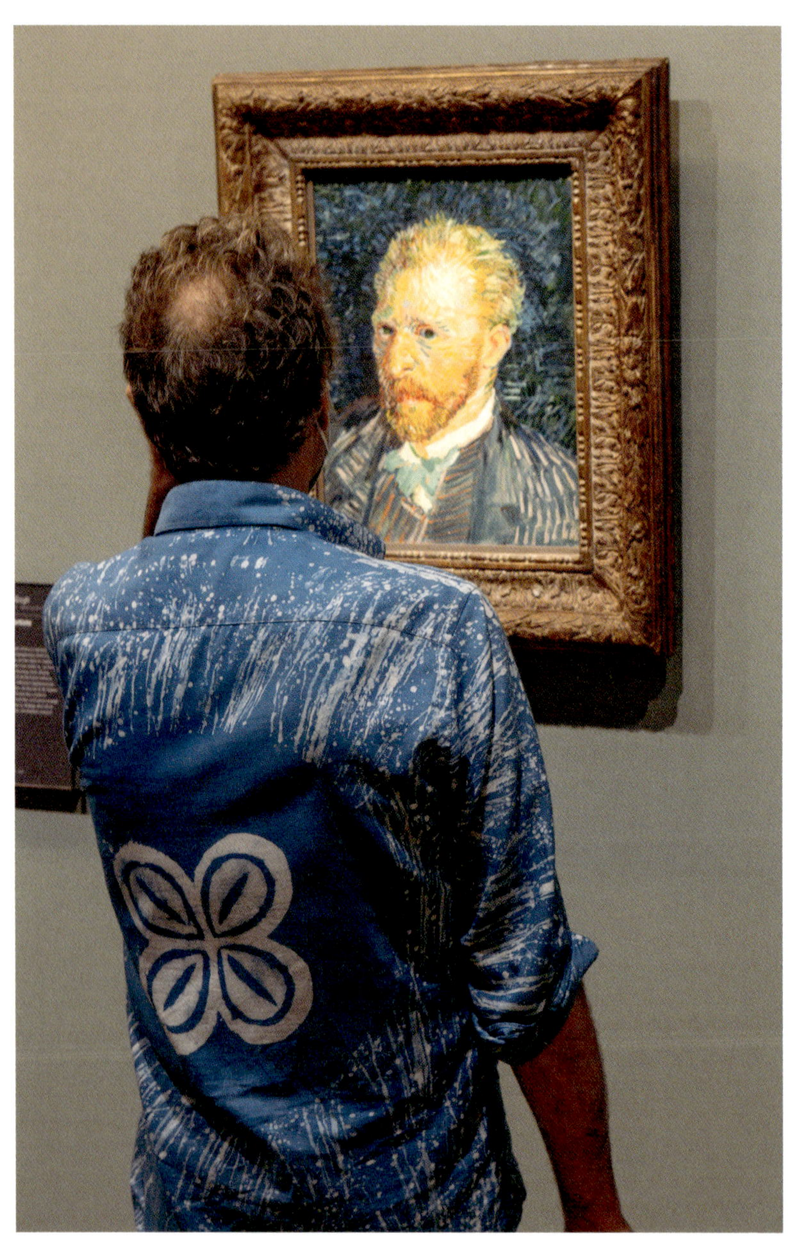

Van Gogh, Musée d'Orsay, Paris

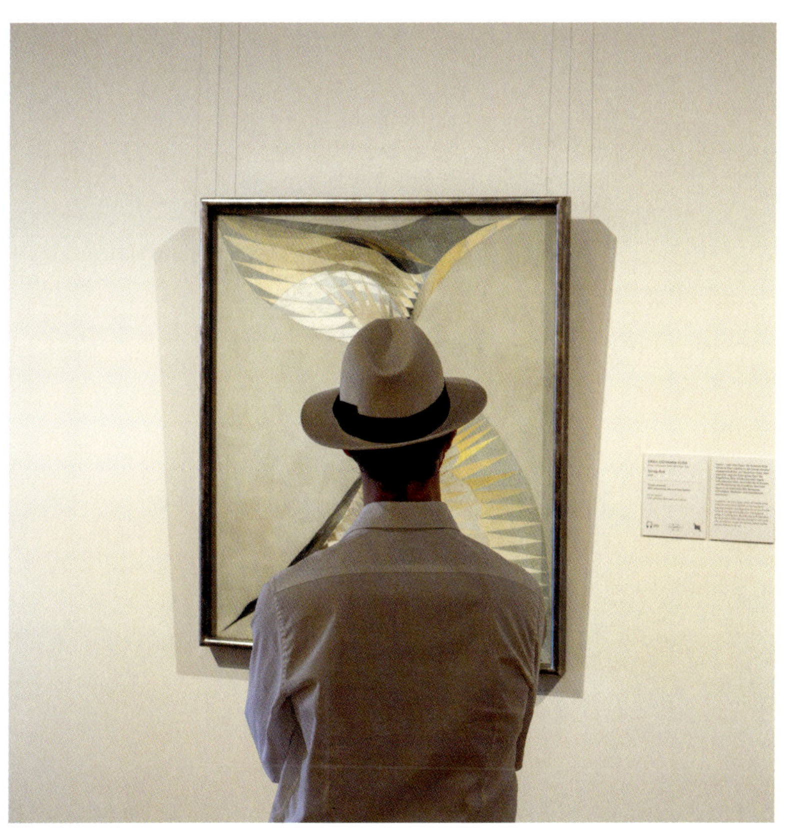

Klien, Österreichische Galerie Belvedere, Vienna

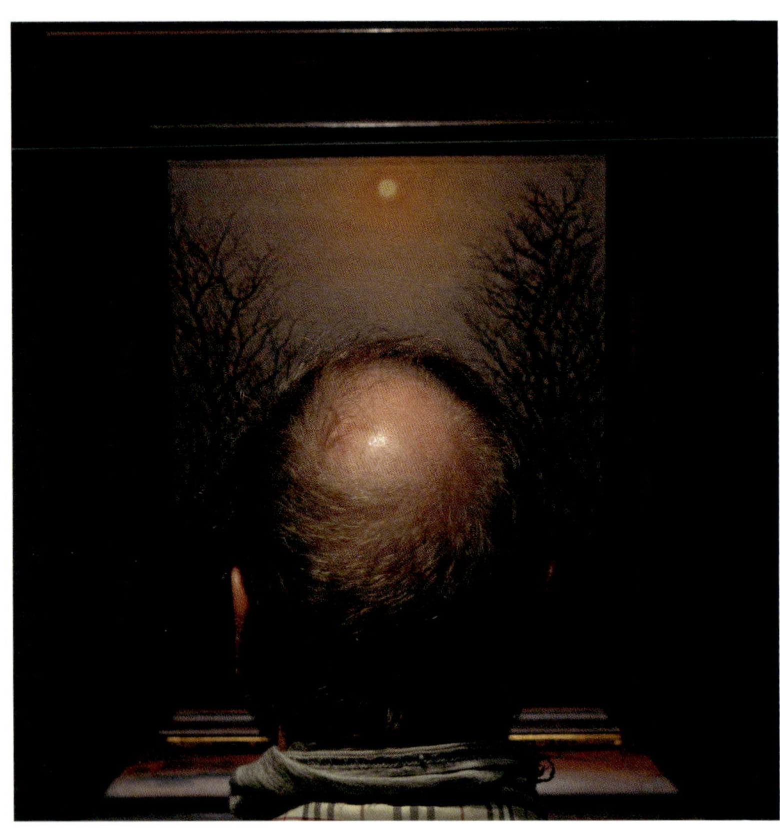

Friedrich, Hamburger Kunsthalle, Hamburg

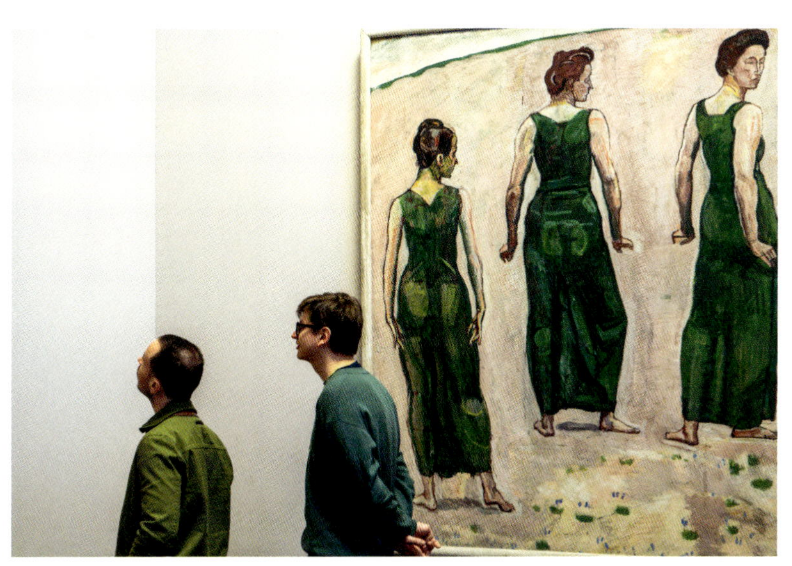

Hodler, Alte Nationalgalerie, Berlin

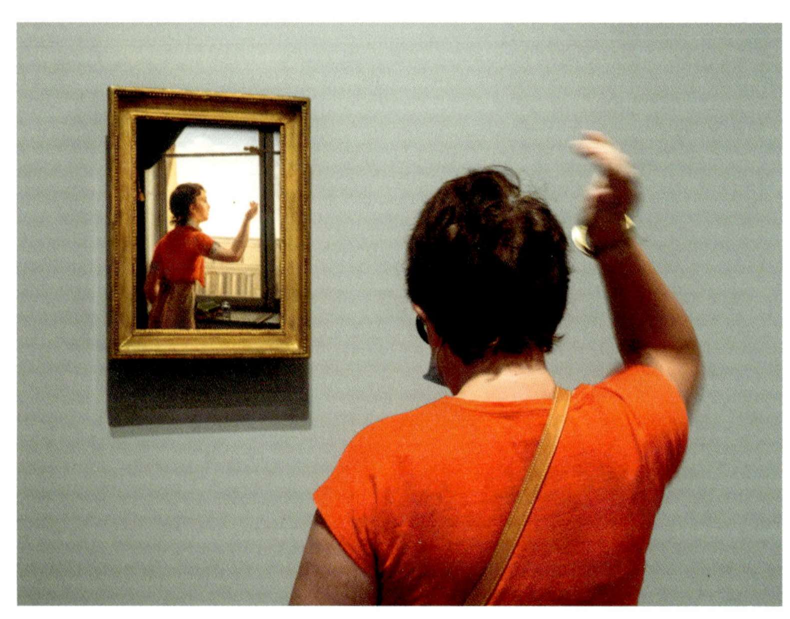

Pinson, Musée du Luxembourg, Paris

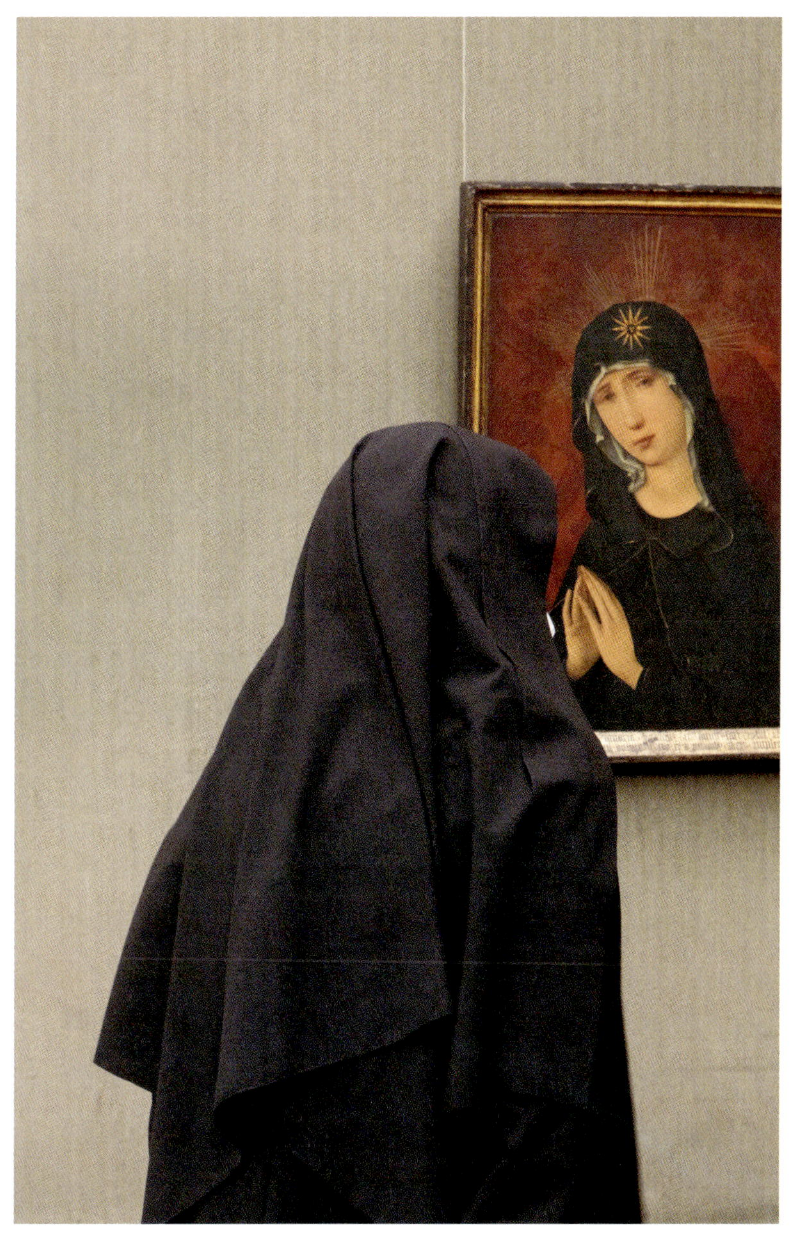

Holbein the Elder, Gemäldegalerie, Berlin

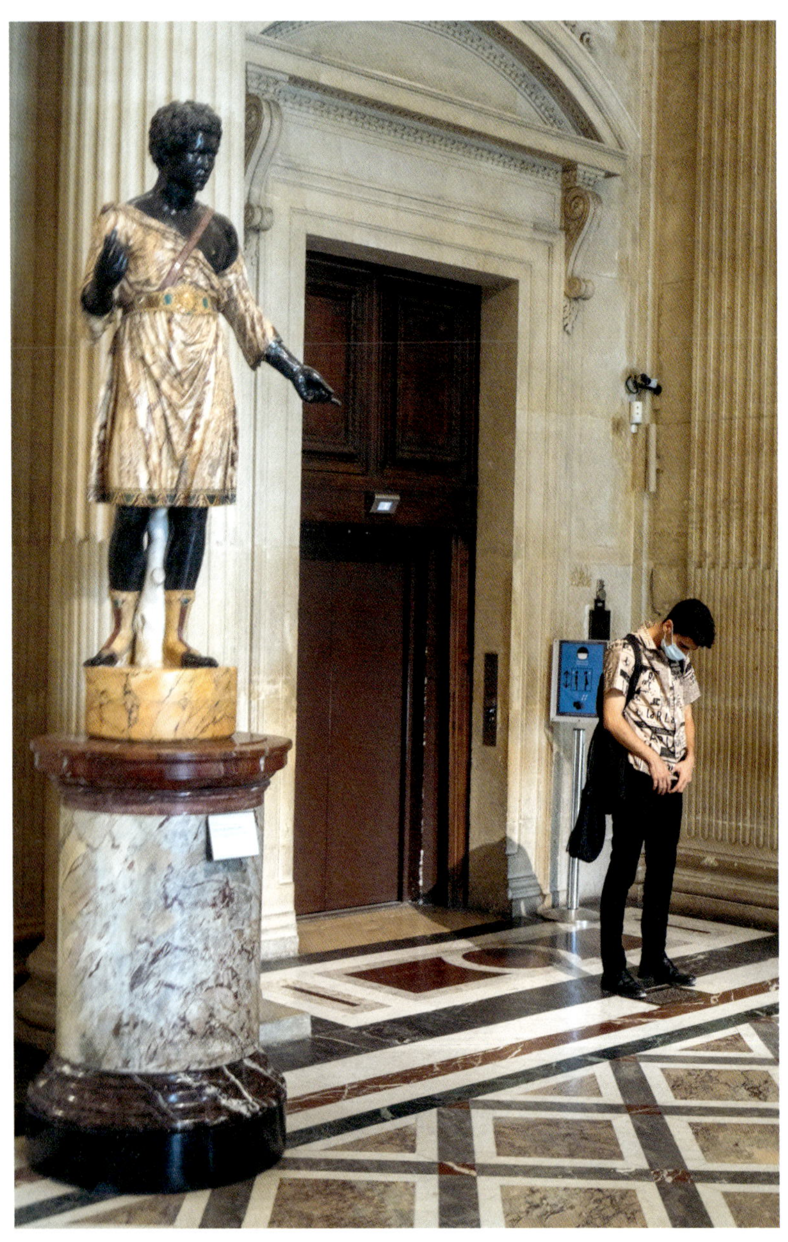

Drouilly, Musée du Louvre, Paris

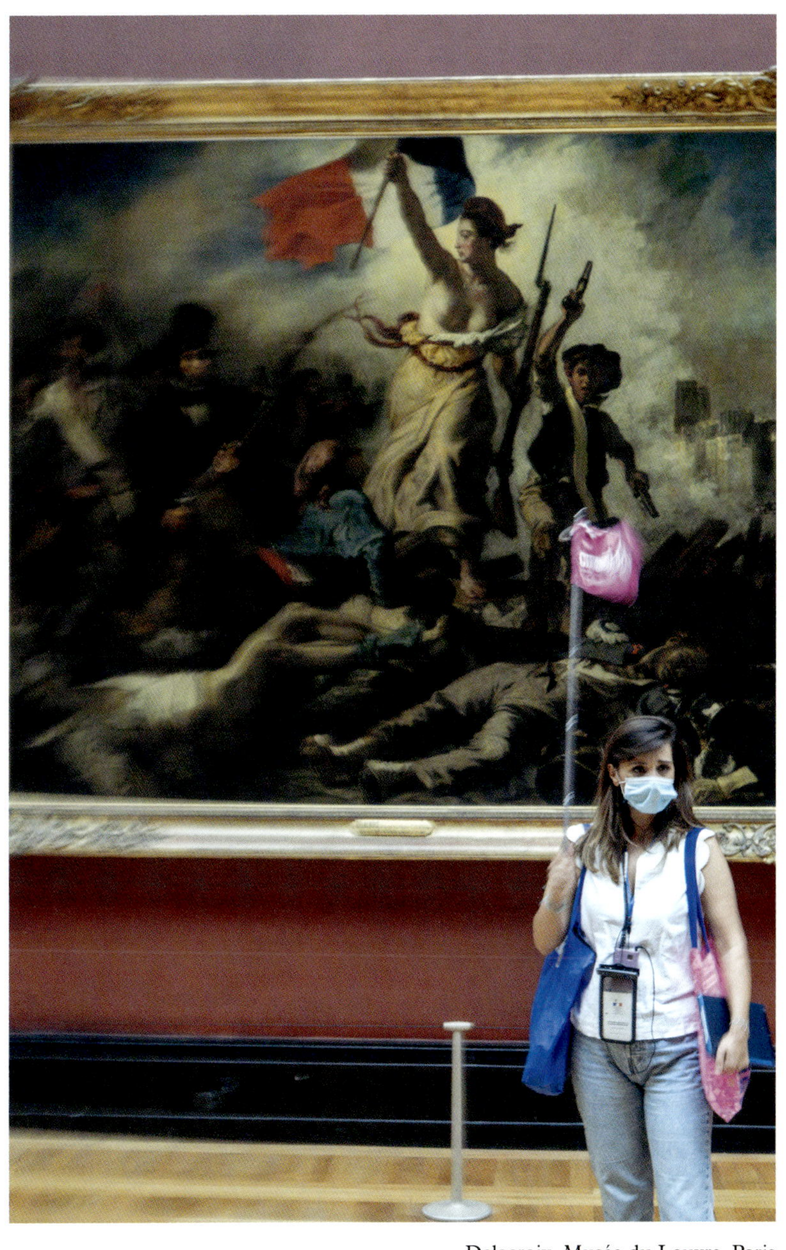

Delacroix, Musée du Louvre, Paris

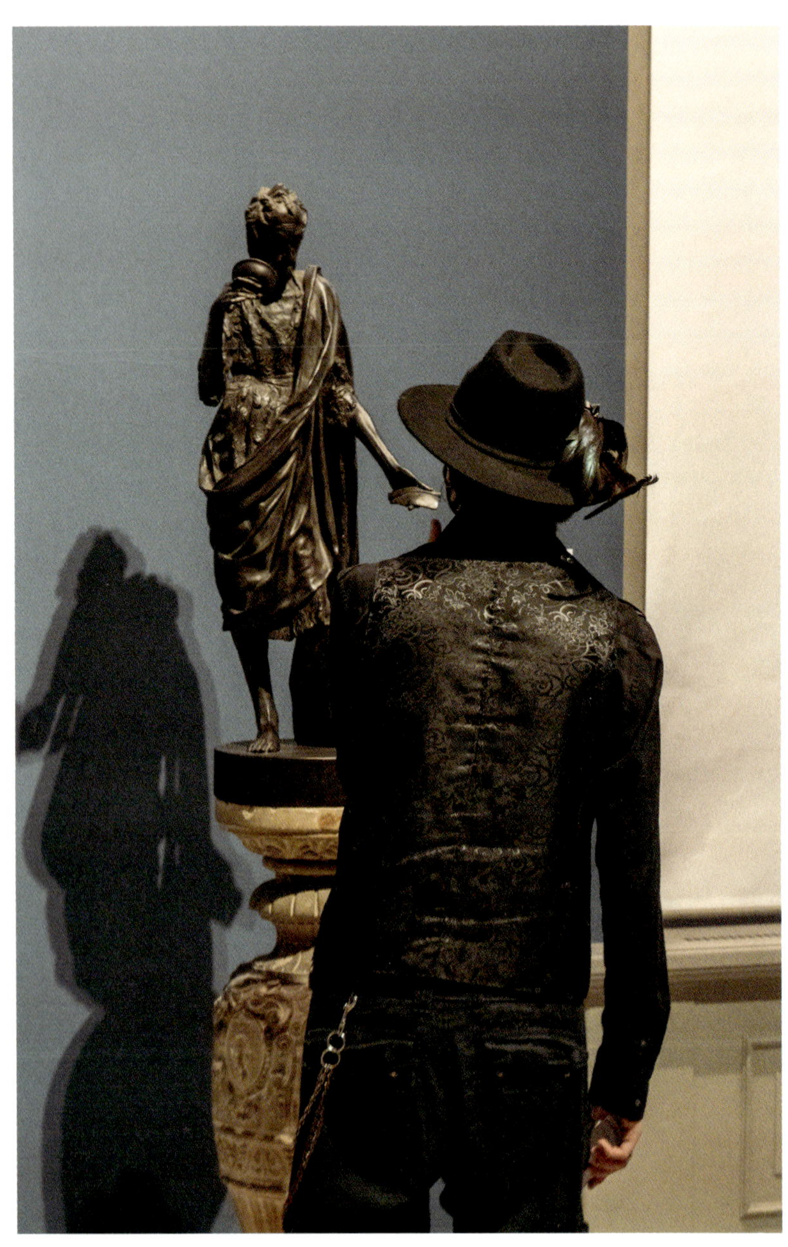

Donatello, Bode-Museum, Berlin

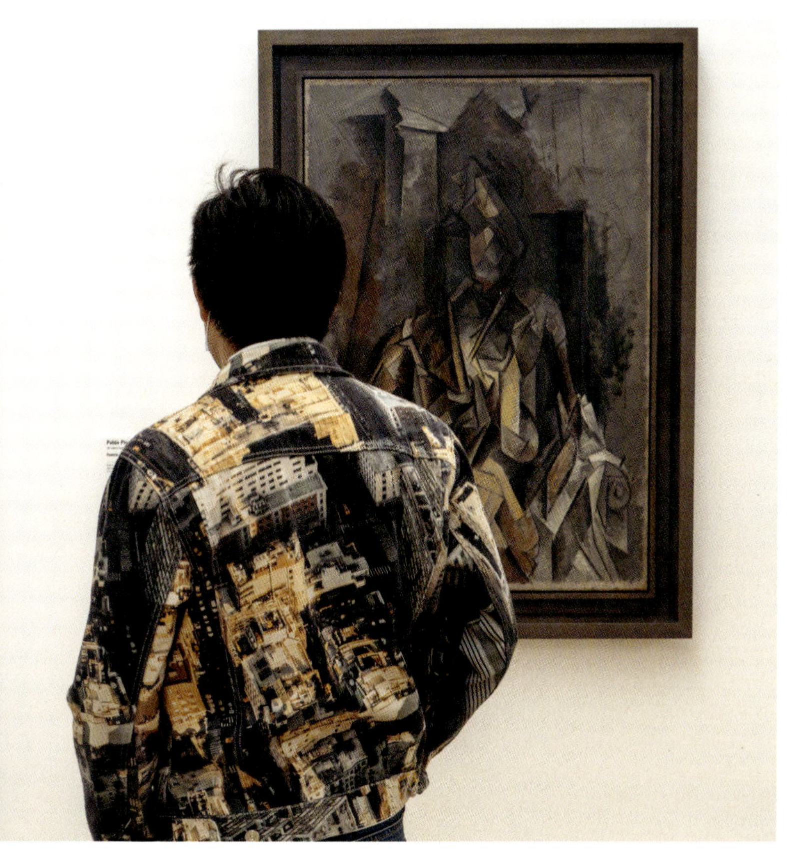

Picasso, Centre Pompidou, Paris

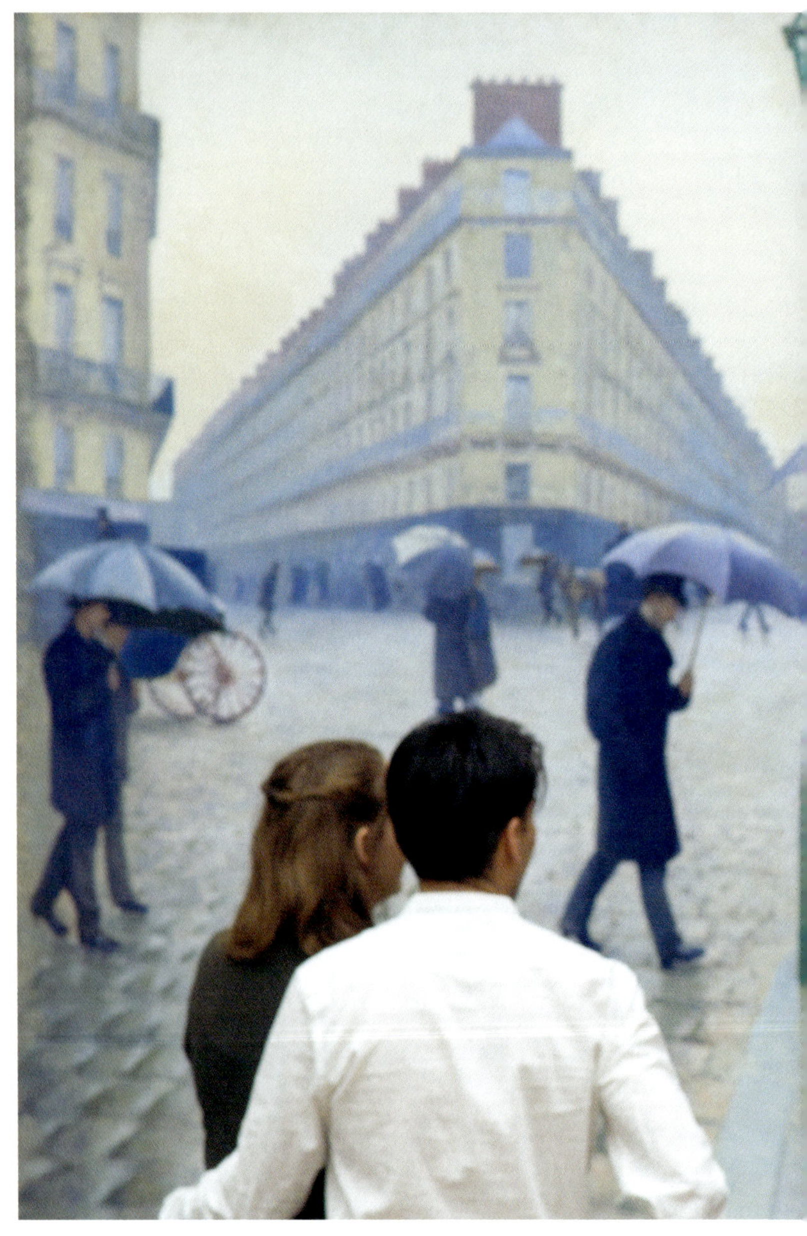

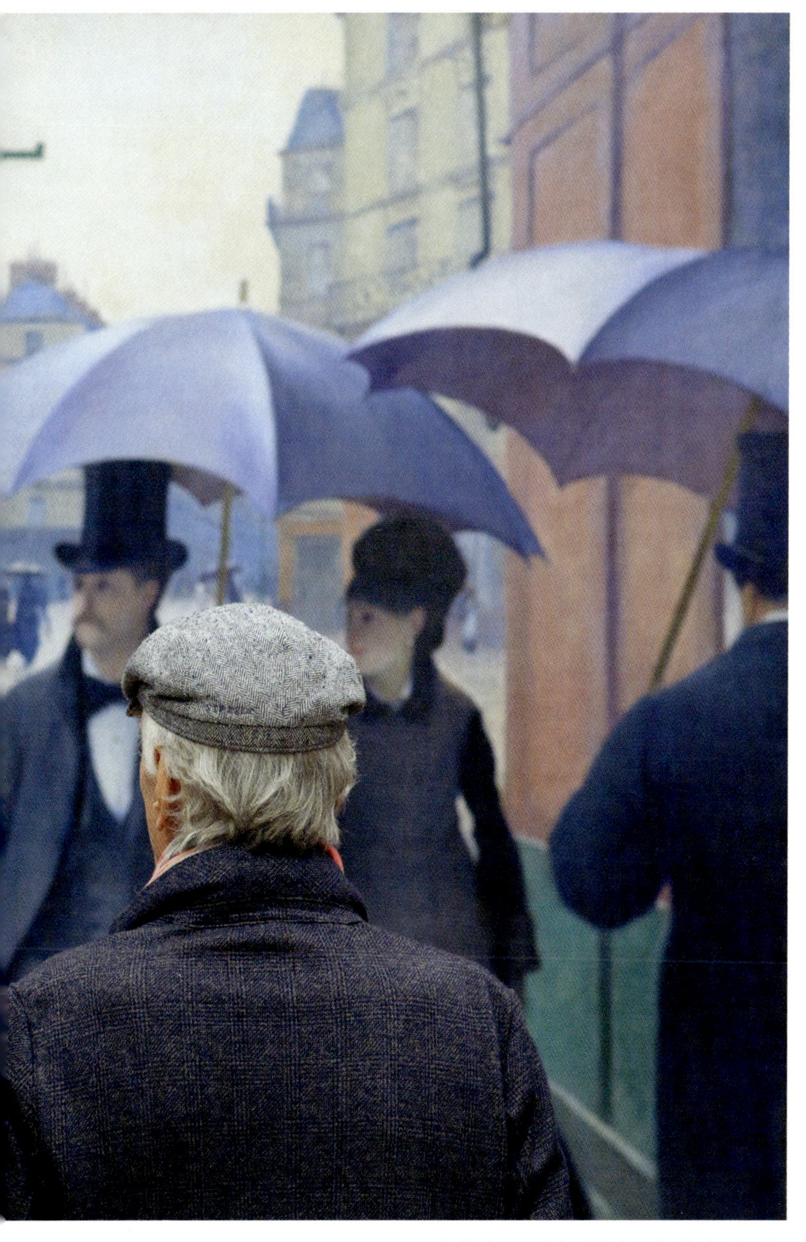

Caillebotte, Alte Nationalgalerie, Berlin

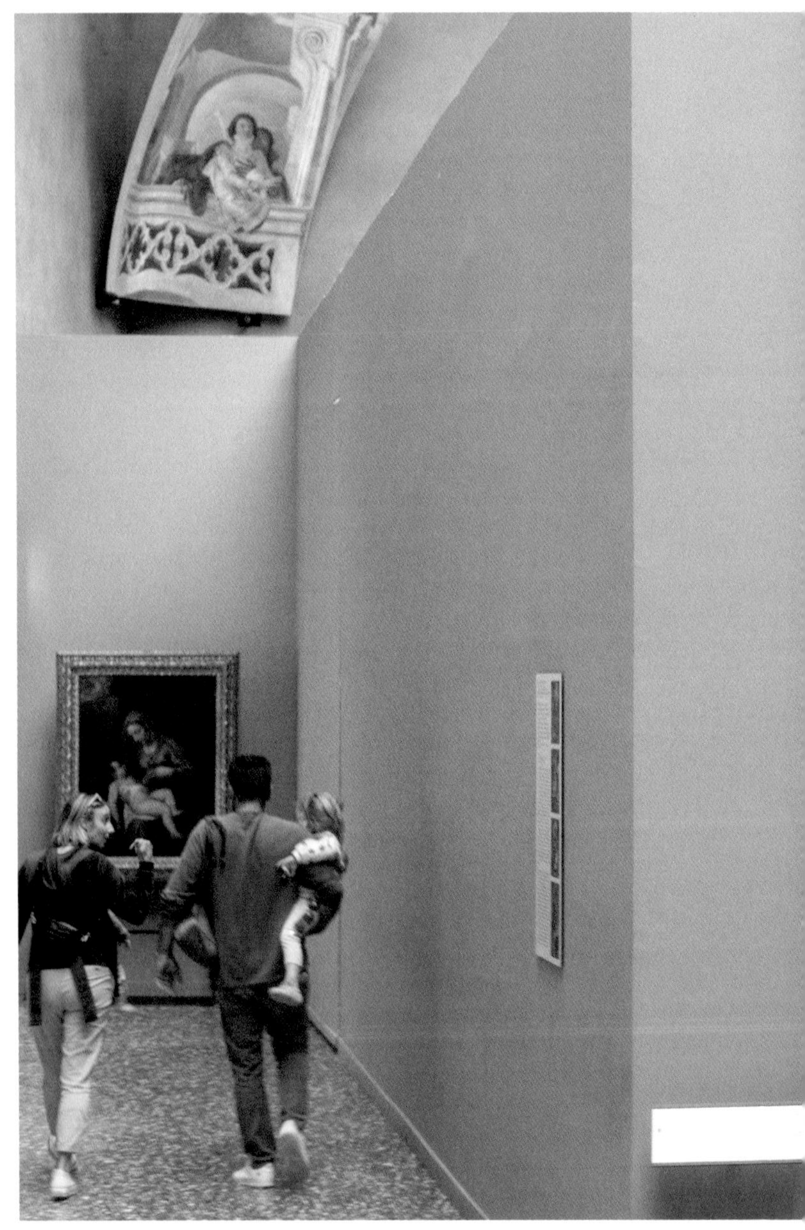

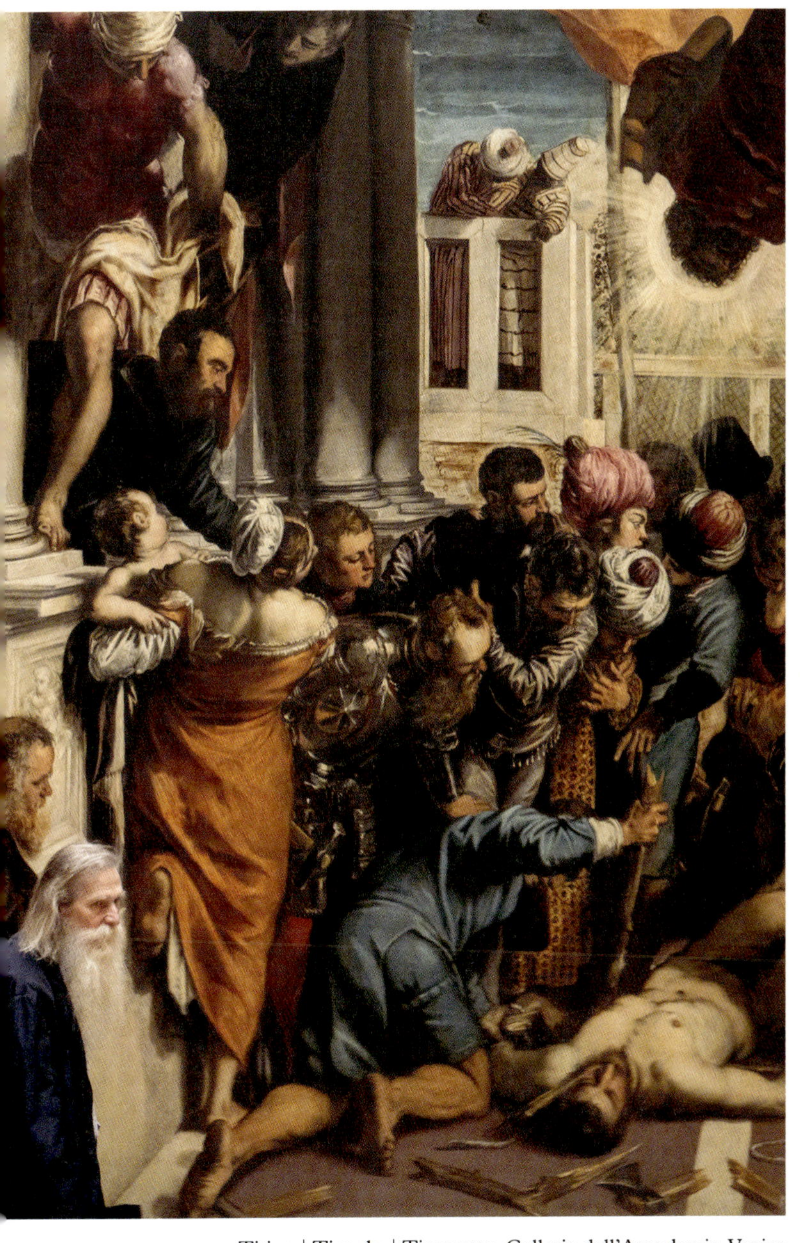

Titian | Tiepolo | Tintoretto, Galleria dell'Accademia, Venice

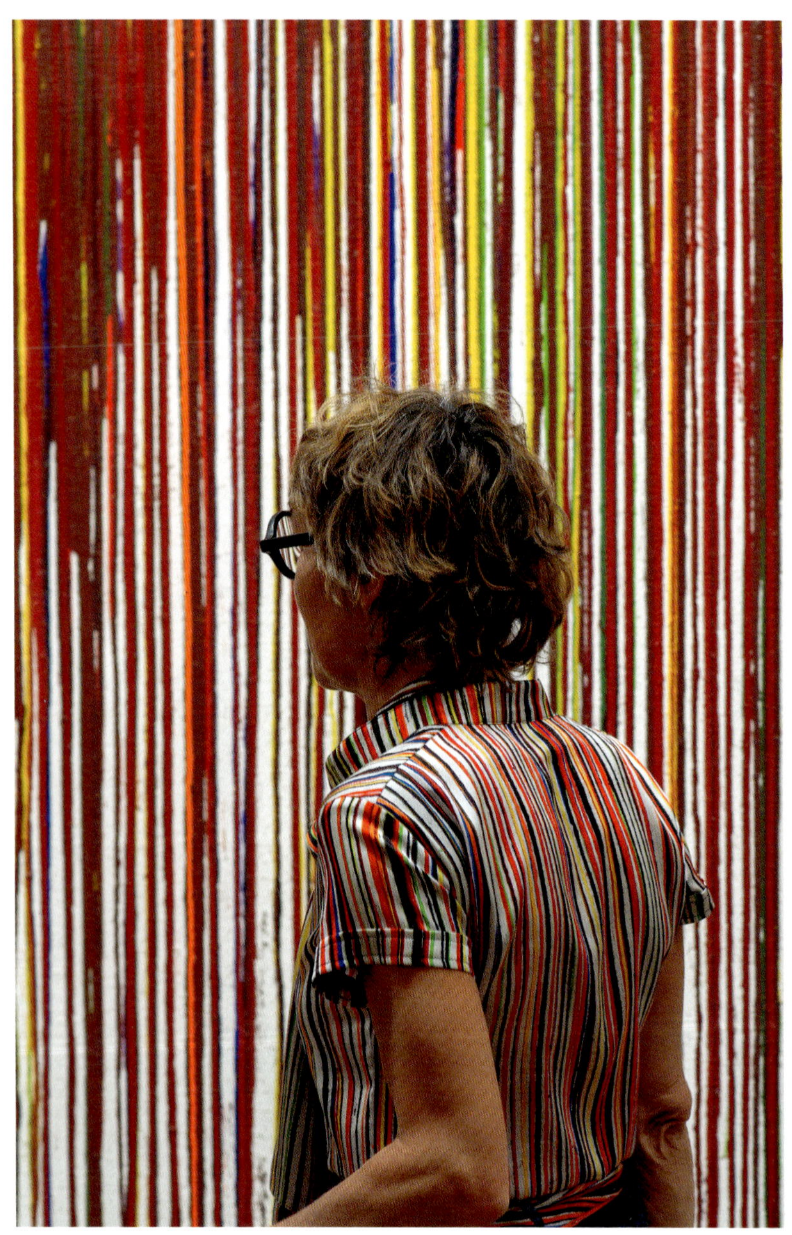

Nitsch, Albertina, Vienna

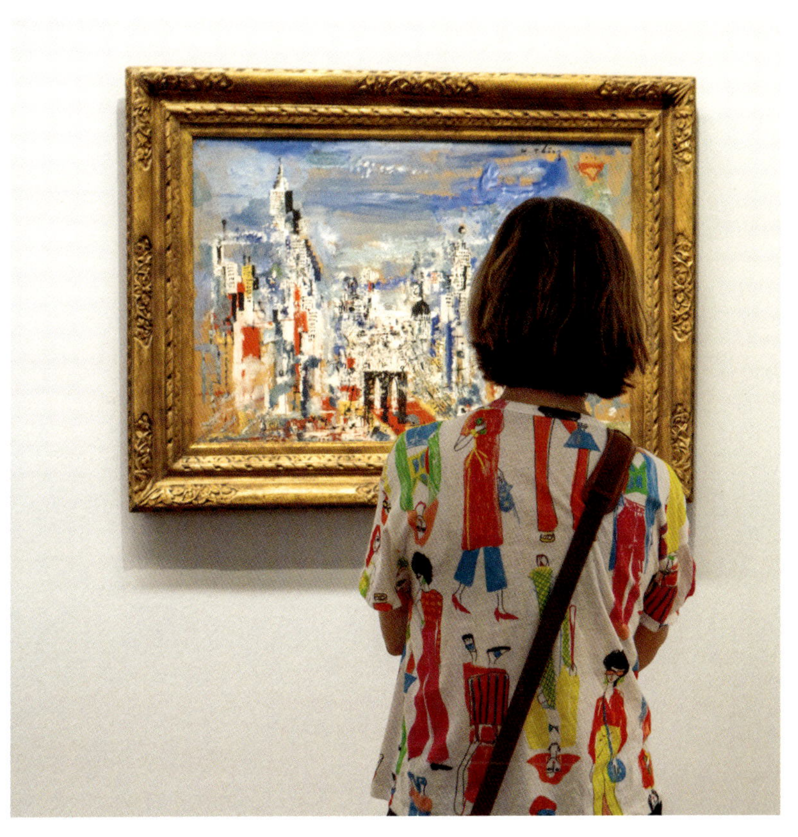

Thöny, Albertina, Vienna

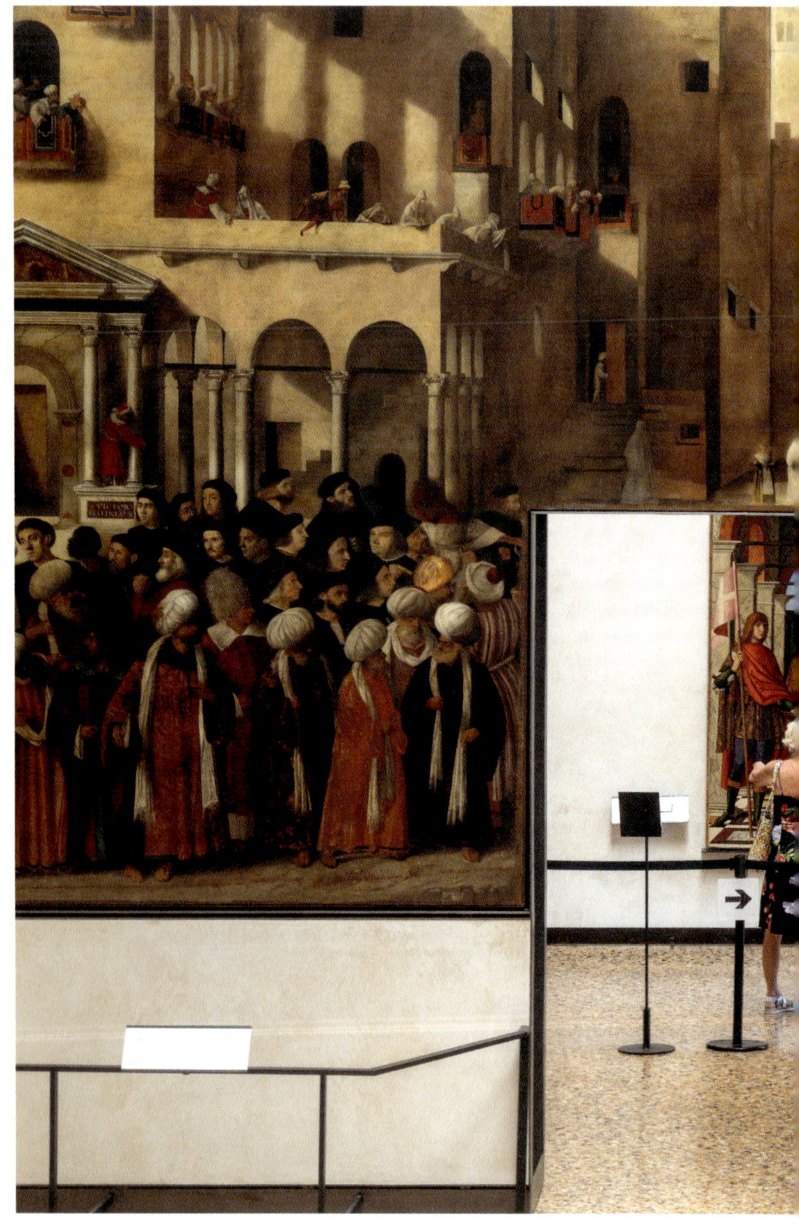

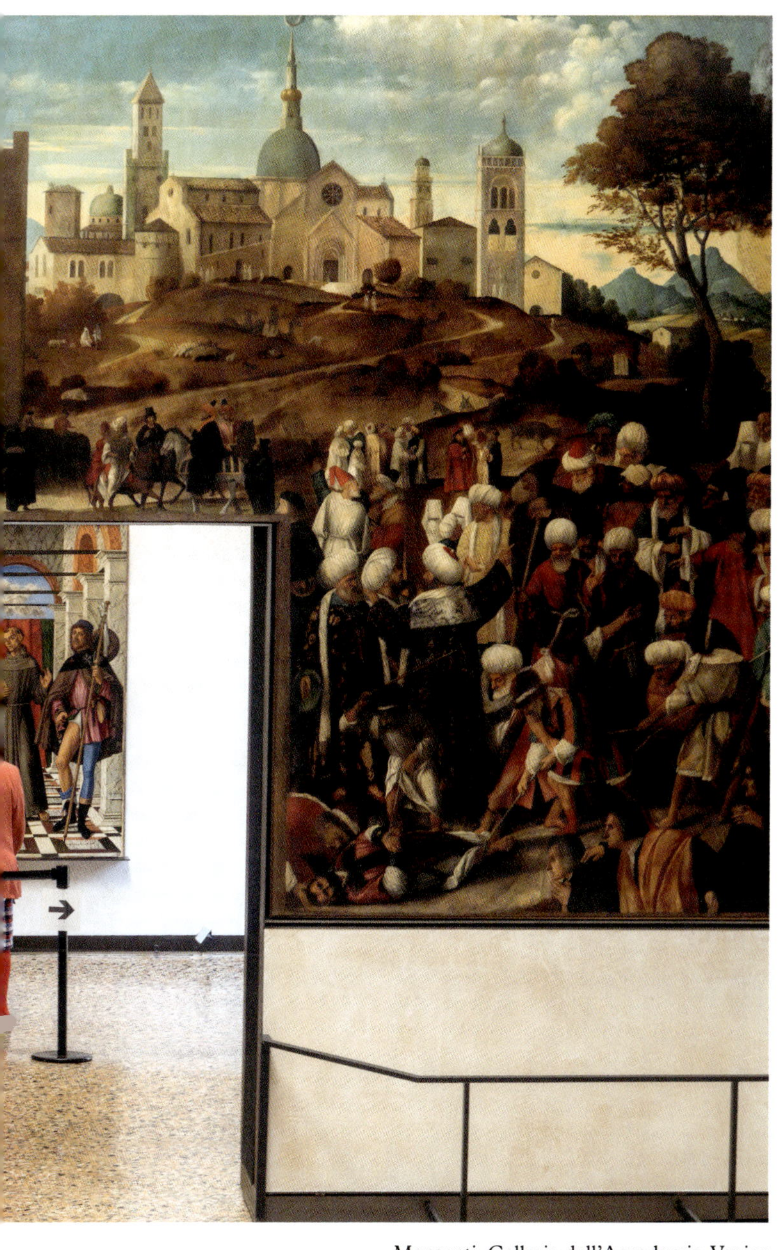

Mansueti, Galleria dell'Accademia, Venice

SLEEPING BEAUTIES
2015–2021

The intense contemplation of art is not a passive affair, but rather a feat of strength. When the French writer Stendhal left the Basilica of Santa Croce in Florence in 1817, he felt his heart pounding: "Life was drained from me. I walked with the fear of falling." It is not surprising, then, that people who feel overwhelmed in museums often take time out.

Intensive Kunstbetrachtung ist keine passive Angelegenheit, eher ein Kraftakt. Als der französische Schriftsteller Stendhal 1817 die Kirche Santa Croce in Florenz verließ, spürte er starkes Herzklopfen, „war bis zum Äußersten erschöpft und fürchtete umzufallen." Kein Wunder also, wenn sich überwältigte Menschen im Museum eine Auszeit nehmen.

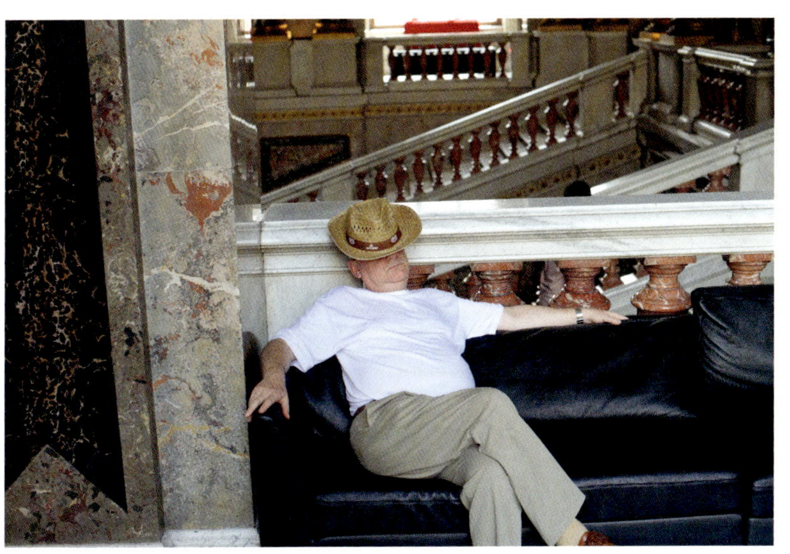

Kunsthistorisches Museum, Vienna

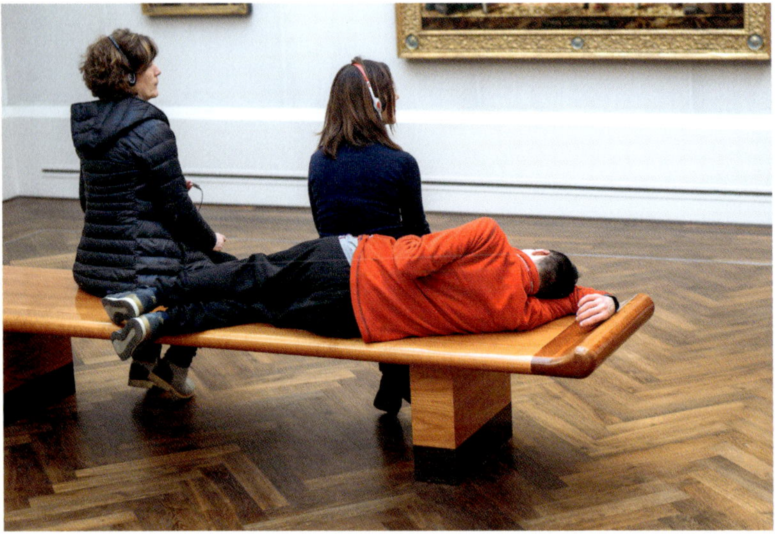

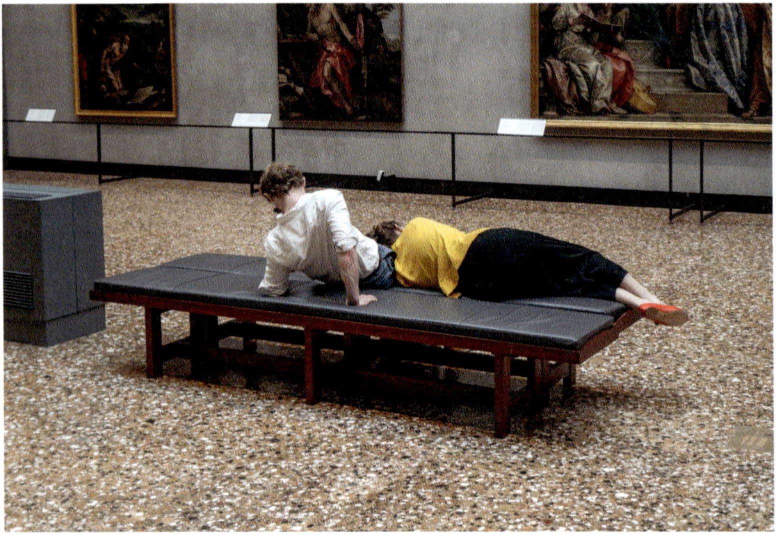

Alte Nationalgalerie, Berlin | Galleria dell'Accademia, Florence

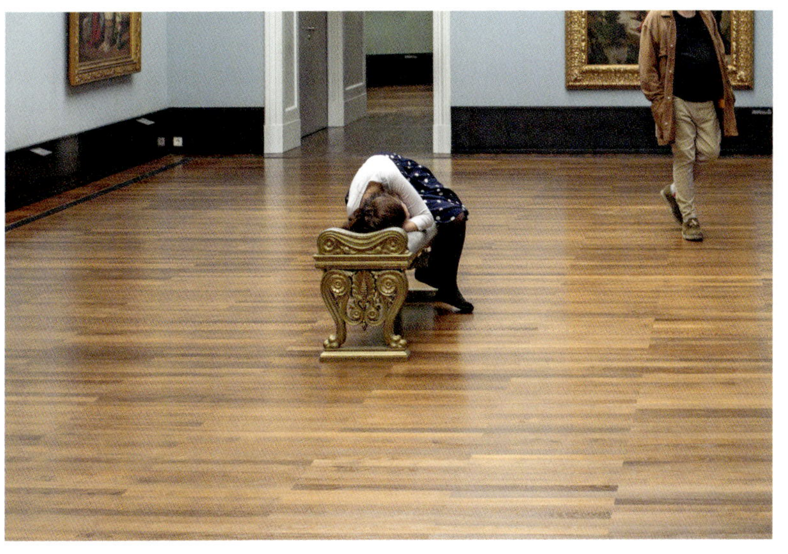

Alte Nationalgalerie, Berlin

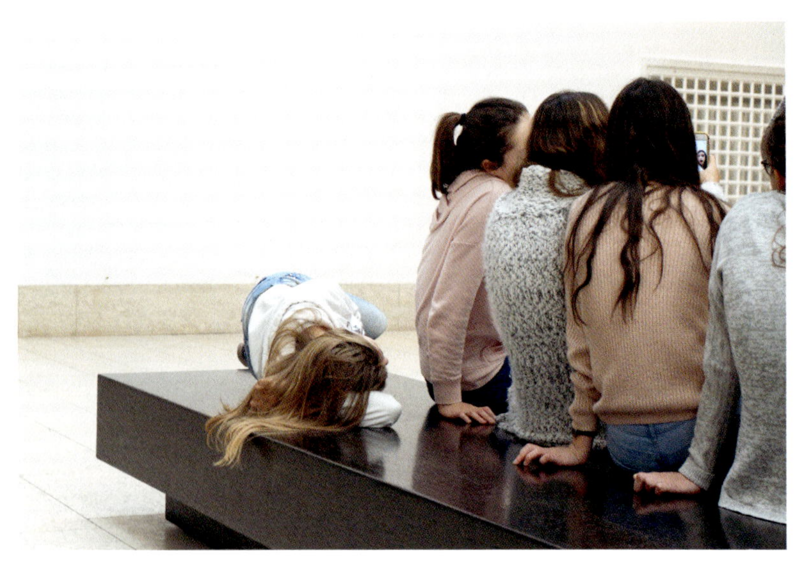

Pergamonmuseum, Berlin

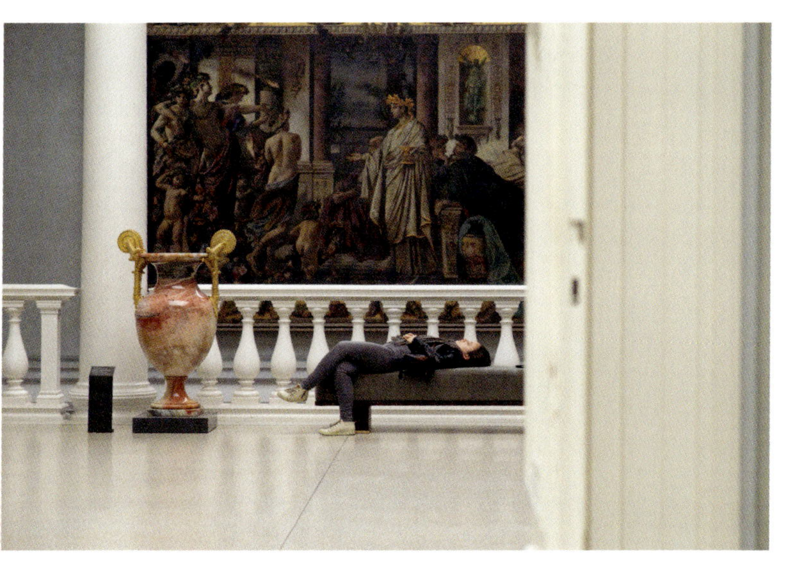

Alte Nationalgalerie, Berlin

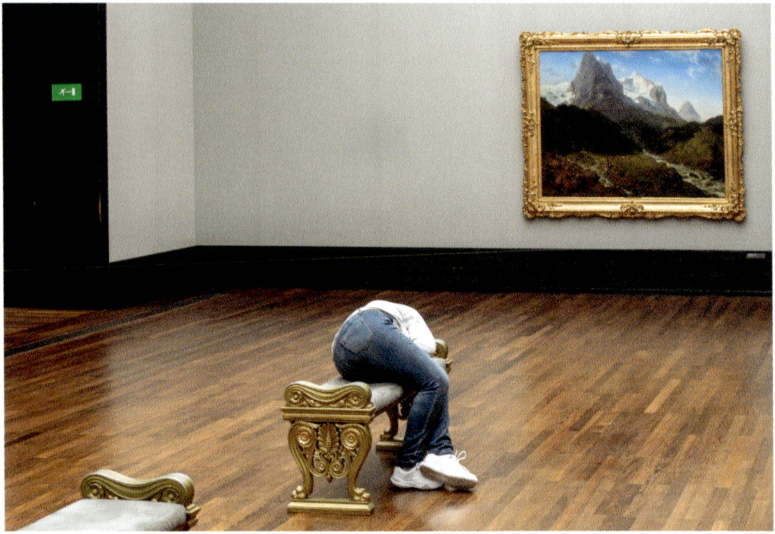

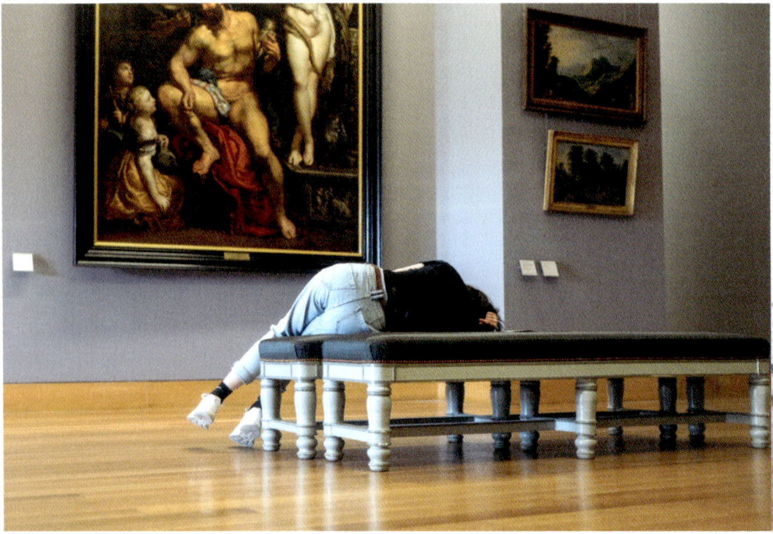

Alte Nationalgalerie, Berlin | Musée du Louvre, Paris

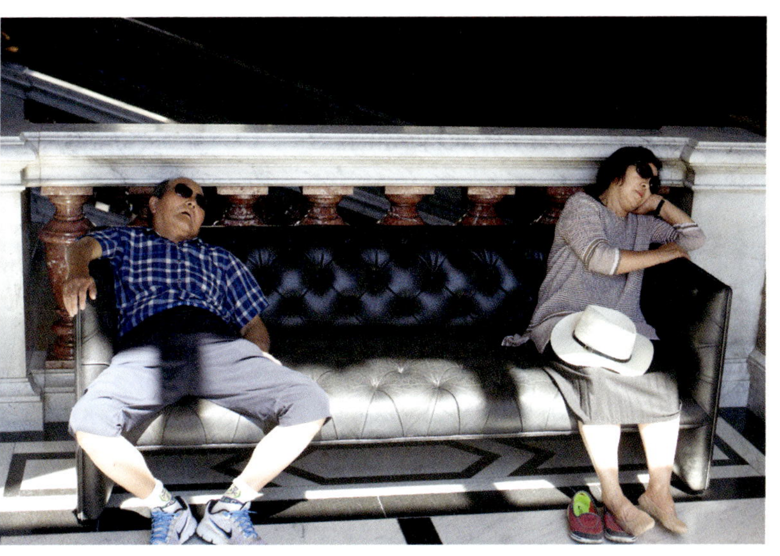

Kunsthistorisches Museum, Vienna

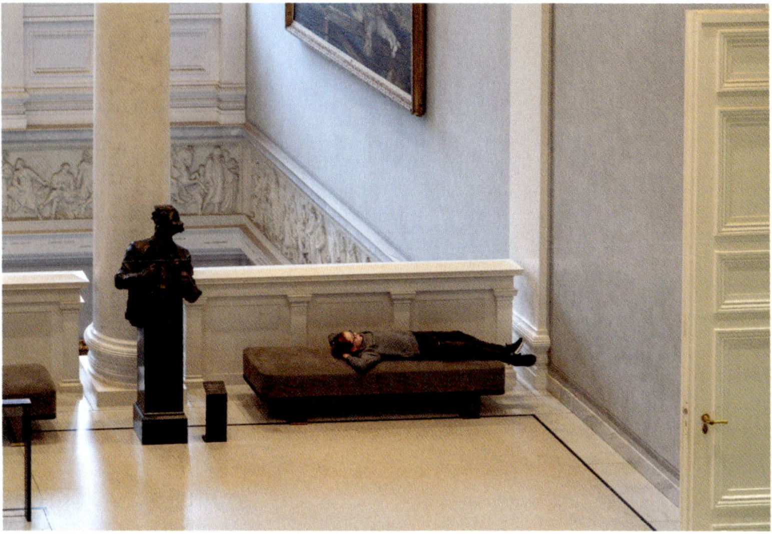

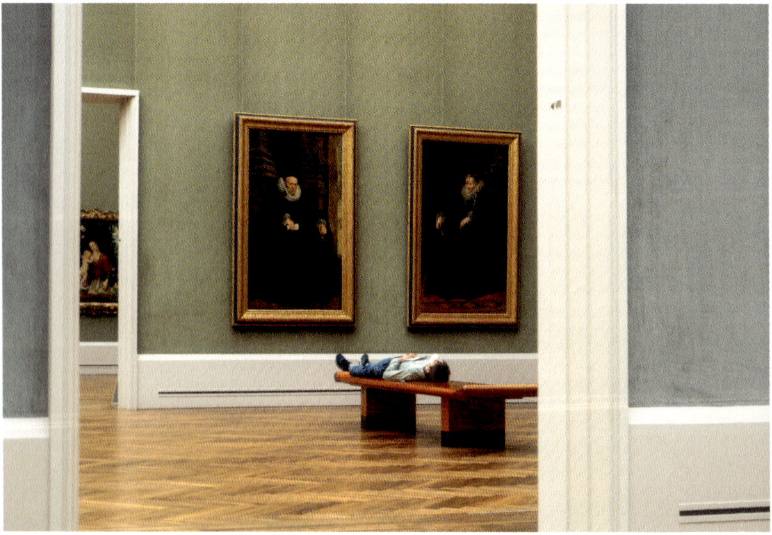

Alte Nationalgalerie, Berlin | Gemäldegalerie, Berlin

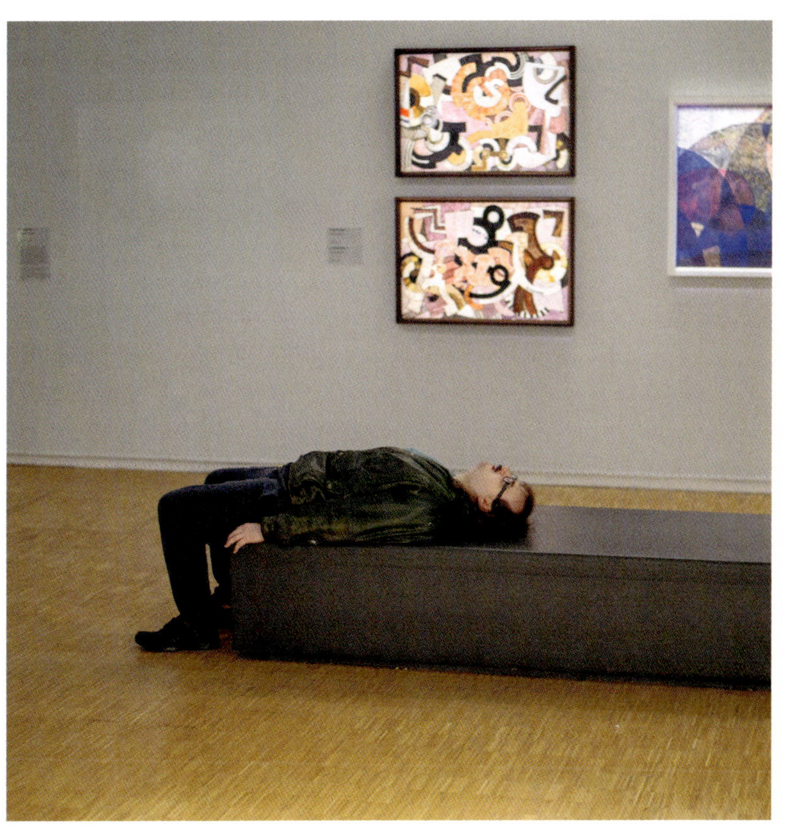

Centre Pompidou, Paris

GESTURES IN MUSEUMS
2015–2022

There are many ways to resonate with works of art—when listening to music, for example, by conducting, singing along, or dancing. As a second-order observer, Stefan Draschan looks at people who react to works of art in museums and who seem just as astonishing as the works themselves.

Es gibt vielfältige Möglichkeiten, mit Kunstwerken in Resonanz zu gehen – beim Musikhören beispielsweise durch Dirigieren, Mitsingen, Tanzen. Als Beobachter zweiter Ordnung betrachtet Stefan Draschan Menschen, die im Museum auf Kunstwerke reagieren und dabei genauso erstaunlich wirken wie die Werke selbst.

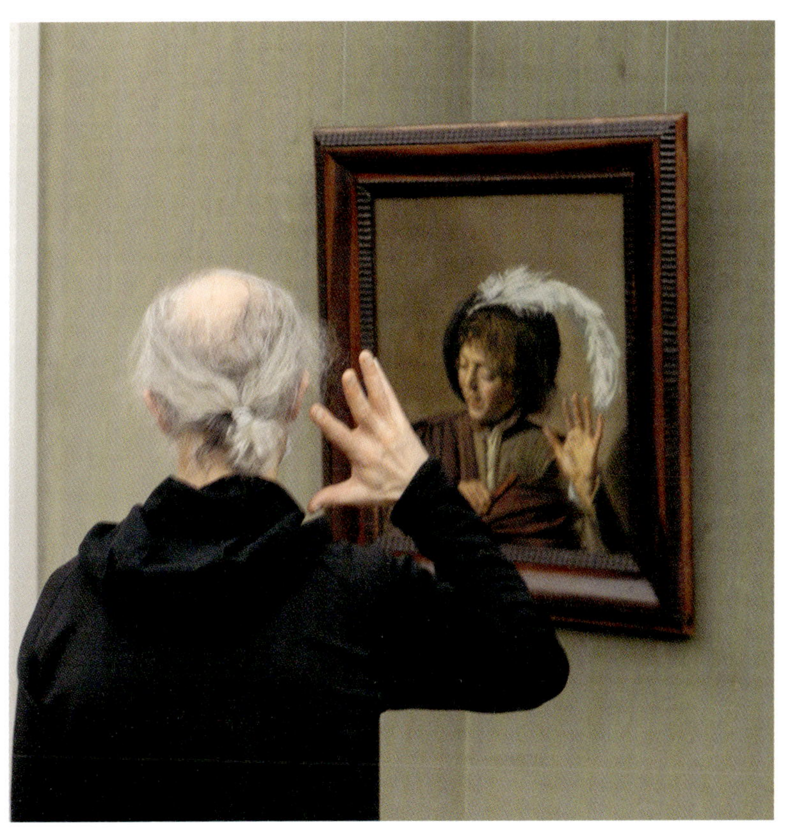

Hals, Gemäldegalerie, Berlin

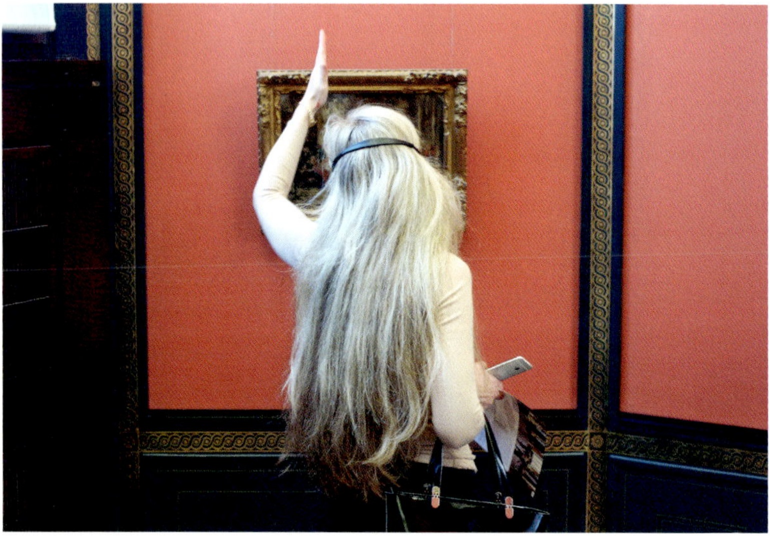

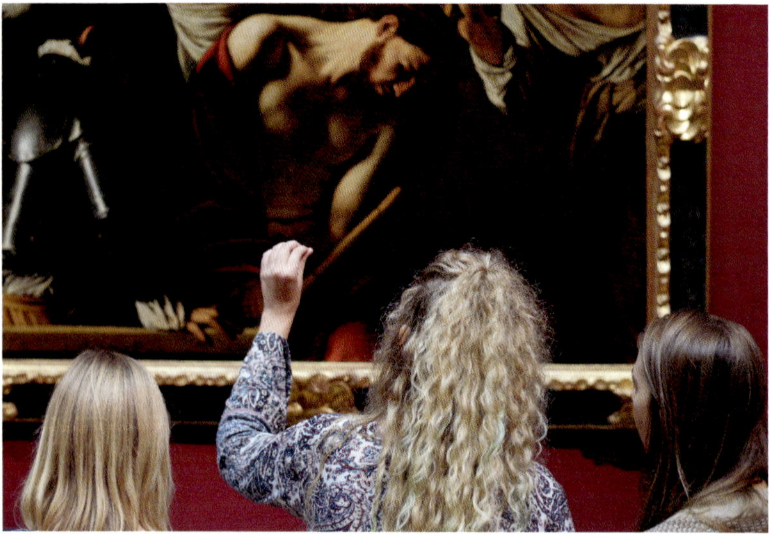

Alte Nationalgalerie, Berlin | Kunsthistorisches Museum, Vienna

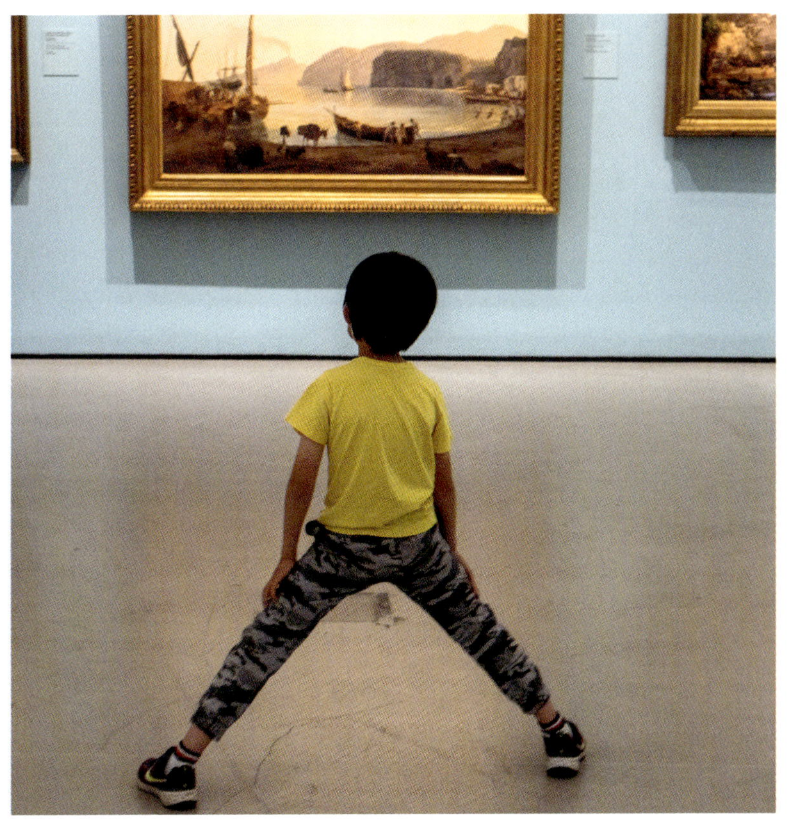

Österreichische Galerie Belvedere, Vienna

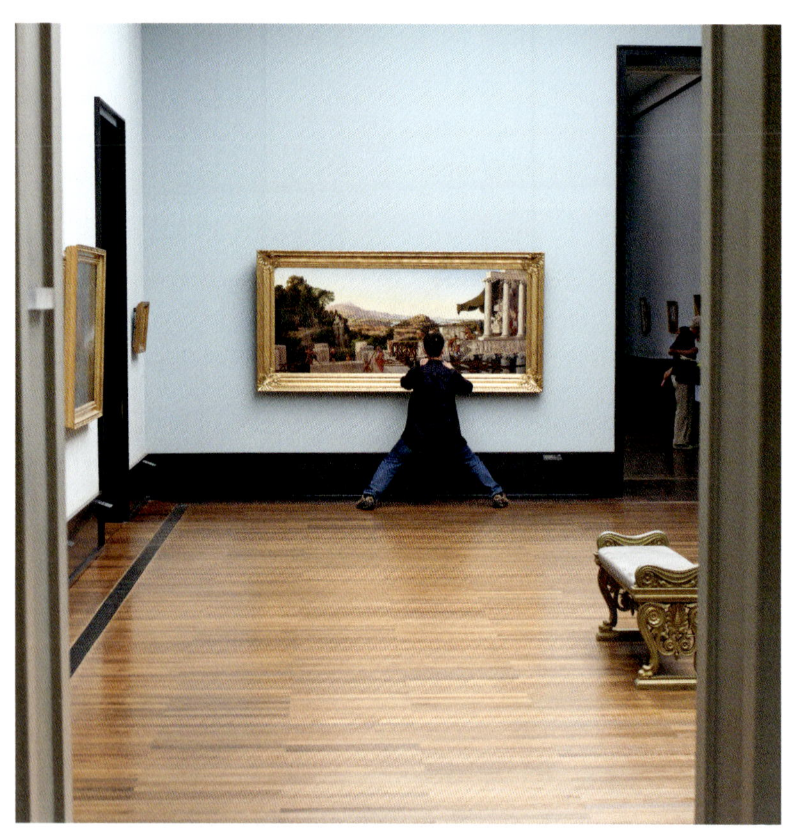

Alte Nationalgalerie, Berlin

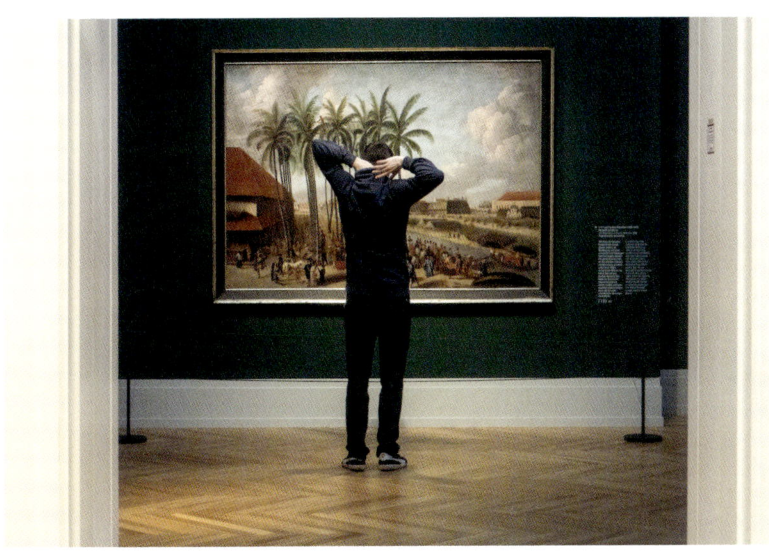

Museum Barberini, Potsdam

007 AT THE MUSEUM
2021–2023

007 in a museum? Absolutely. In *Skyfall*, Her Majesty's secret agent visits the National Gallery in London and gazes wistfully at William Turner's *The Fighting Temeraire* (1839), a decommissioned battleship. In *Spectre*, Modigliani's painting entitled *Woman with a Fan* (1919), which was stolen from a Paris museum in 2010, reappears. And in *Dr. No*, Bond discovers—on second glance—Goya's portrait of the Duke of Wellington, which went missing from the National Gallery in 1961.

007 im Museum? Definitiv. In Skyfall *besucht der Geheimagent seiner Majestät die National Gallery in London und betrachtet melancholisch William Turners* The Fighting Temeraire *(1839) – ein ausrangiertes Schlachtschiff. In* Spectre *taucht Modiglianis Bild einer* Frau mit Fächer *(1919) wieder auf, das 2010 aus einem Pariser Museum entwendet wurde. Und in* Dr. No *entdeckt Bond – beim zweiten Hinsehen – Goyas Porträt des Duke of Wellington, das 1961 der National Gallery abhandenkam.*

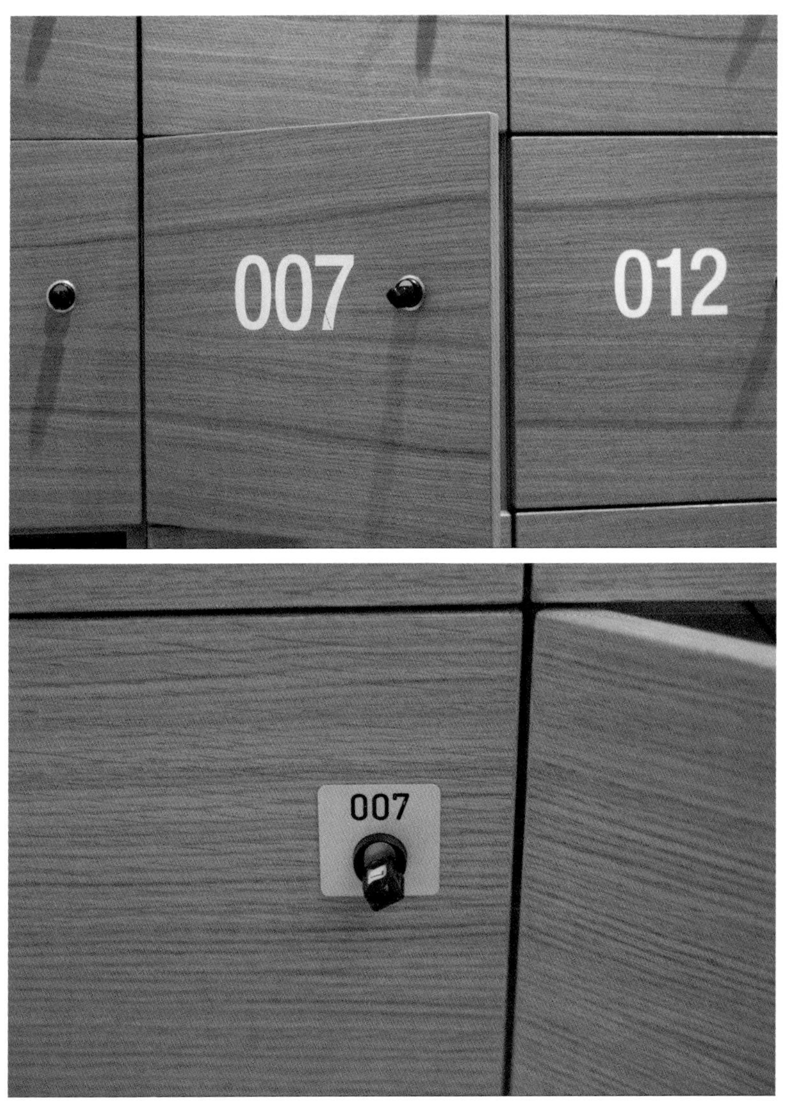

Österreichische Galerie Belvedere, Vienna | Albertina, Vienna

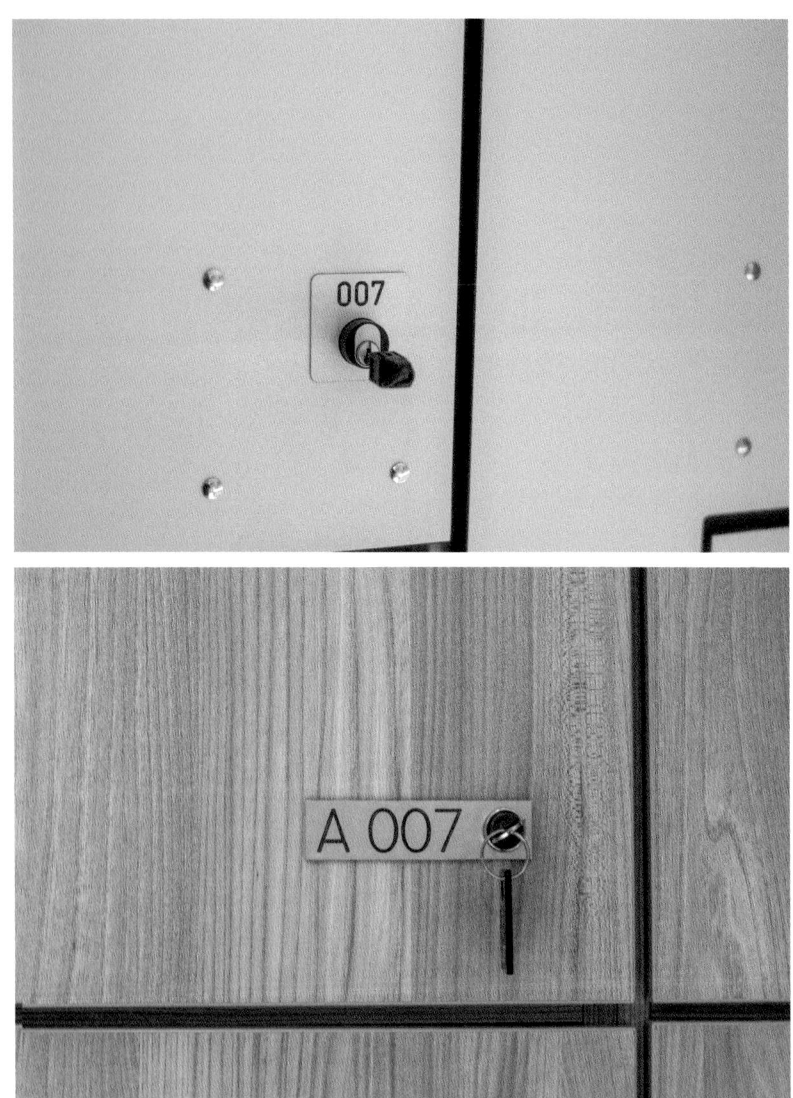

Sammlung Scharf-Gerstenberg, Berlin | Museum of Fine Arts, Budapest

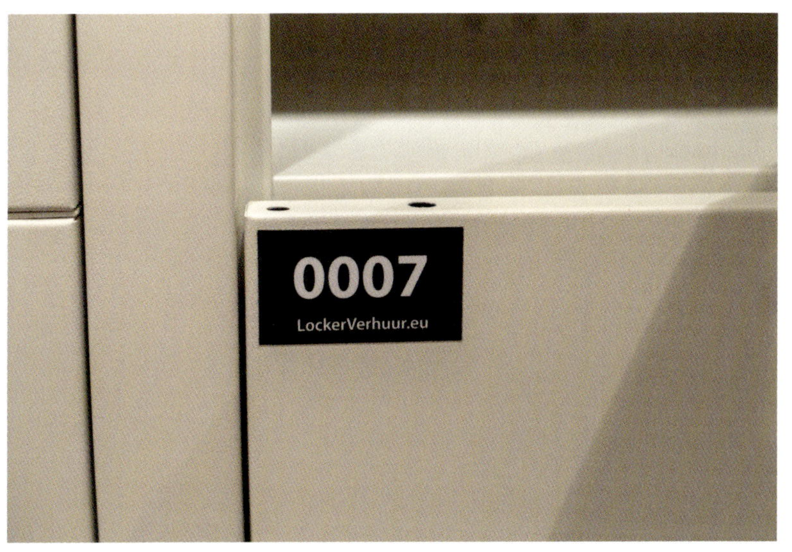

Rijksmuseum, Amsterdam

MUSEUMS OF WATER 2015–2021

The museum is a high-tech security zone with air conditioning, motion detectors, and security guards, but above all it is a world of signs and symbols. Water damage is a sudden intrusion of the real. It is astonishing how archaically it is dealt with, with the improvised installation of buckets in rows, on wheels, or surrounded by their own stanchion barriers.

Das Museum ist eine Hightech-Sicherheitszone mit Klimaanlage, Bewegungsmeldern und Wachpersonal, vor allem jedoch eine Welt der Zeichen und Symbole. Der Wasserschaden ist ein plötzlicher Einbruch des Realen. Erstaunlich, wie archaisch ihm begegnet wird, mit der improvisierten Installation von Auffangbehältern in Serie, auf Rädern oder umgeben von eigenen Absperrungen.

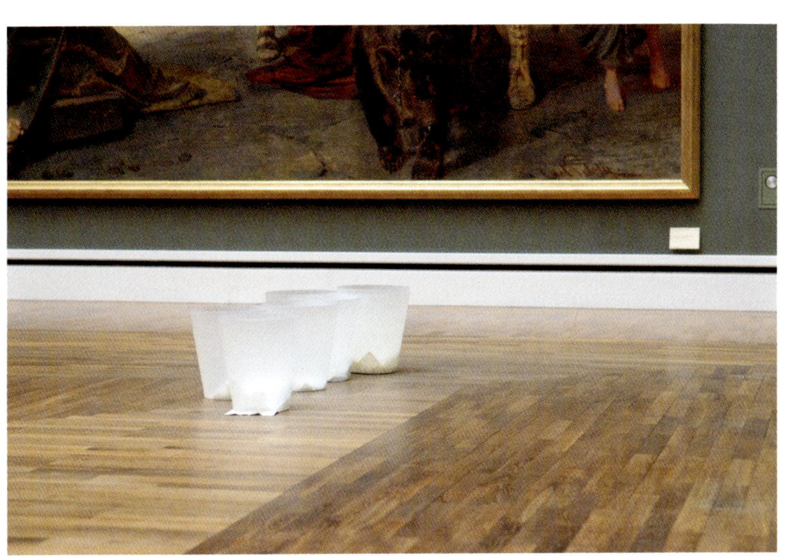

Pinakothek, Munich

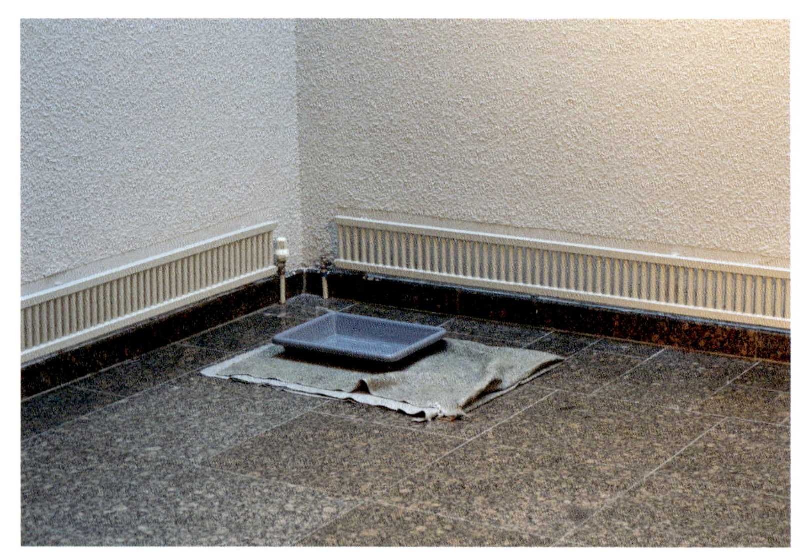

Kunstgewerbemuseum, Berlin

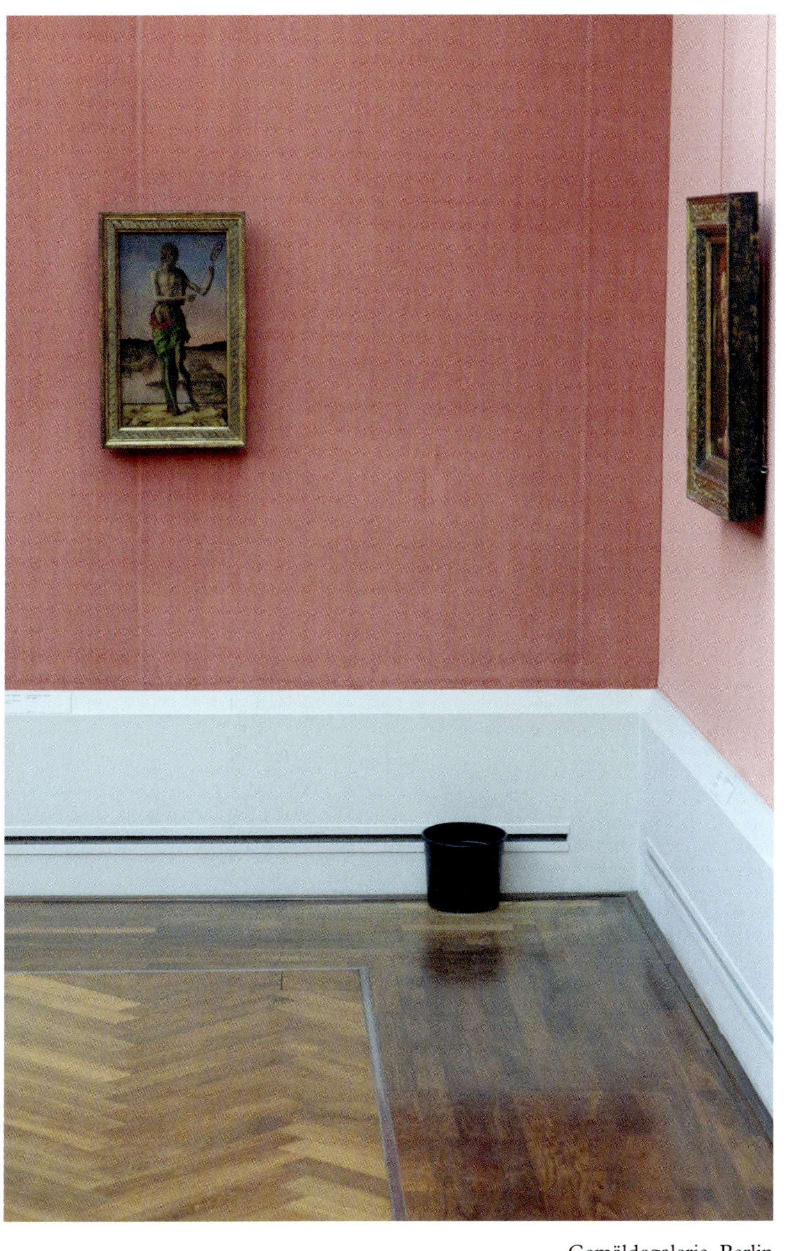

Gemäldegalerie, Berlin

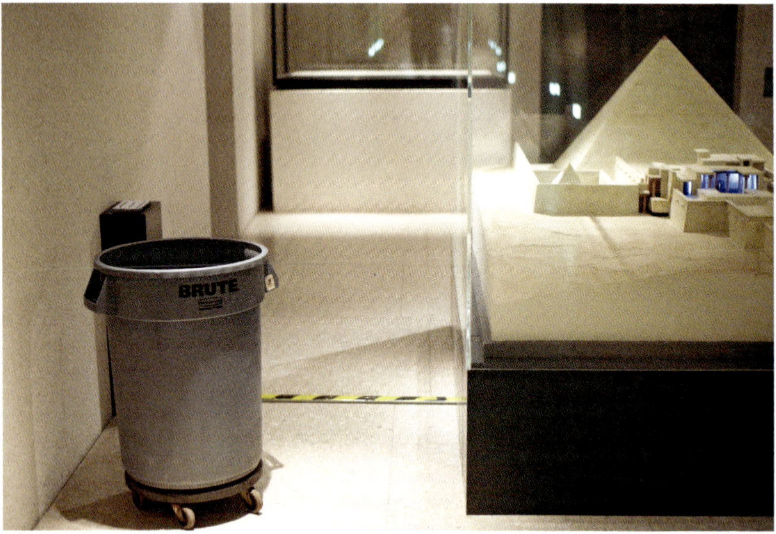

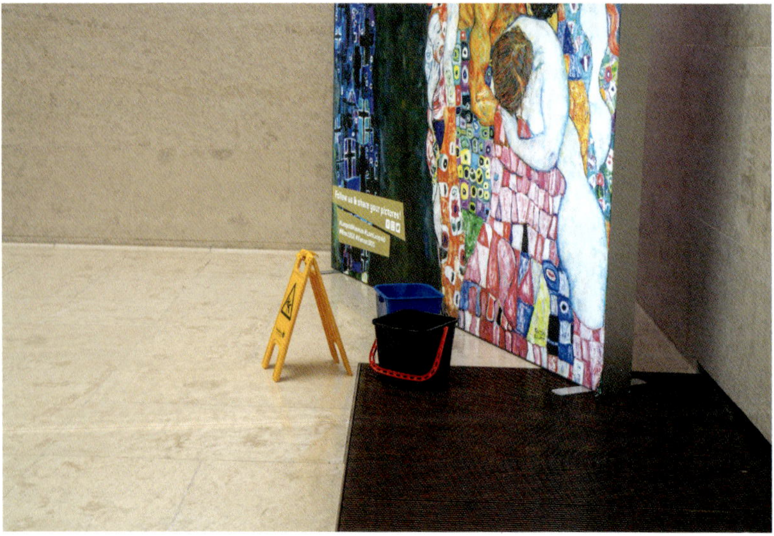

Altes Museum, Berlin | Leopold Museum, Vienna

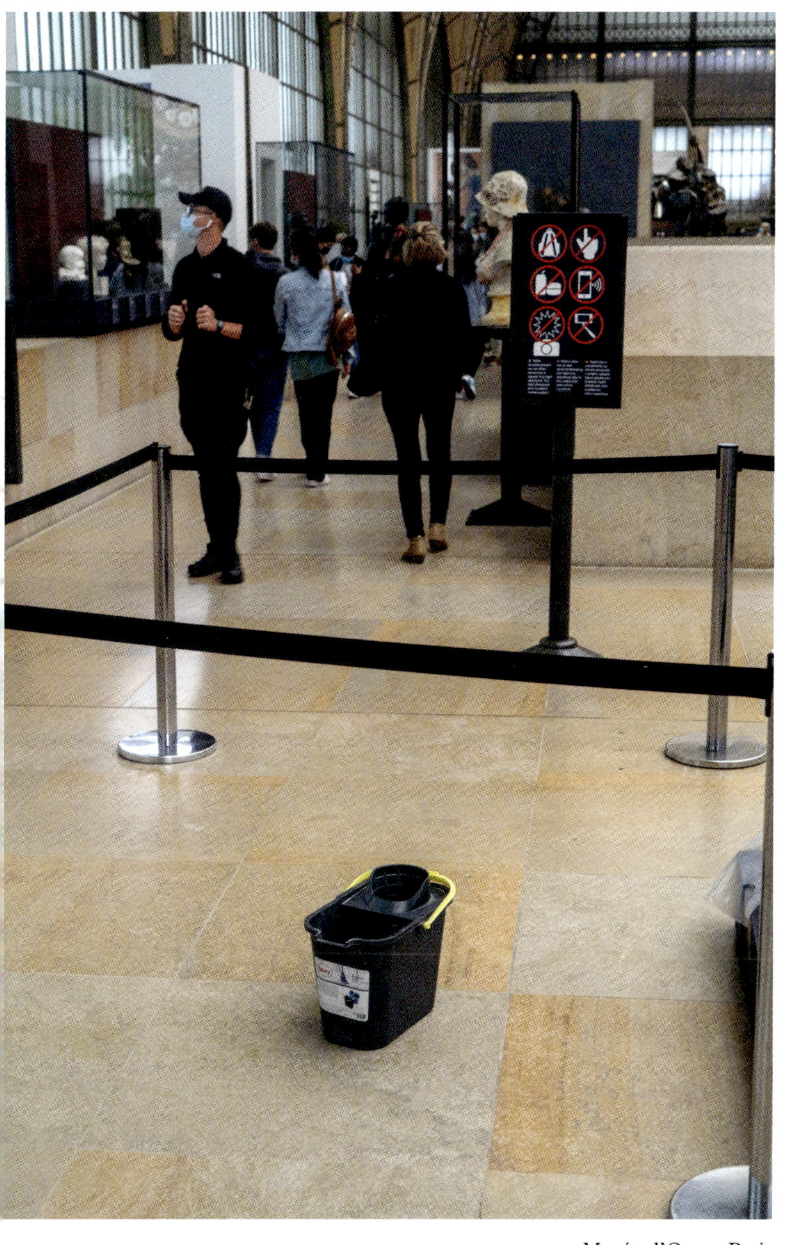

Musée d'Orsay, Paris

DOUBLE TAKE
2015–2021

A “double take” is the opposite of “swipe and click,” the art of the second glance, of a renewed, more thorough, even literally oblique look, whether with the aid of instruments such as a magnifying glass or binoculars, or with the simplest of means: marking out a section of a picture with the thumb and forefinger of both hands.

Ein „Double Take“ ist das Gegenteil von Wischen-und-Klicken, die Kunst des zweiten Blicks, der erneuten, gründlicheren, sogar buchstäblich geneigten Betrachtung – sei es unter Einsatz von Instrumenten wie Lupe oder Fernglas, sei es mit einfachsten Mitteln: die Begrenzung eines Bildausschnitts durch Daumen und Zeigefinger beider Hände.

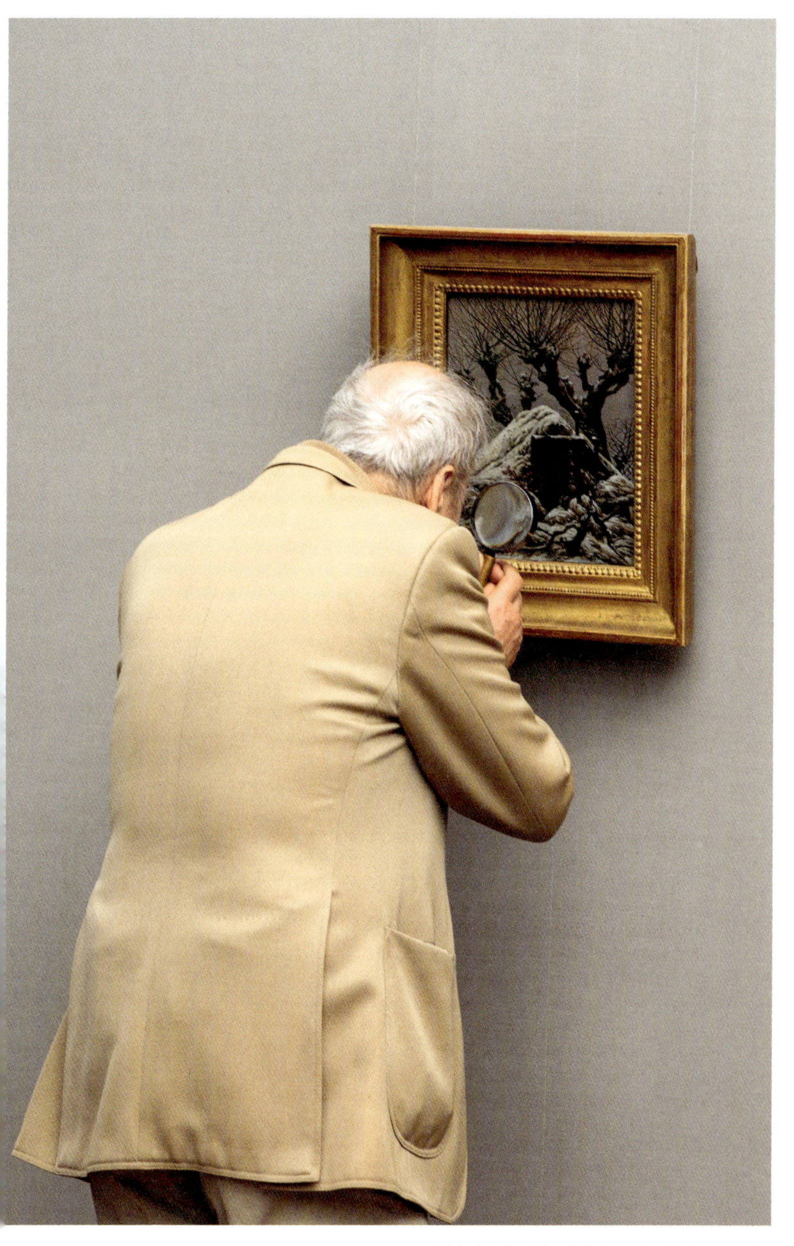

Friedrich, Alte Nationalgalerie, Berlin

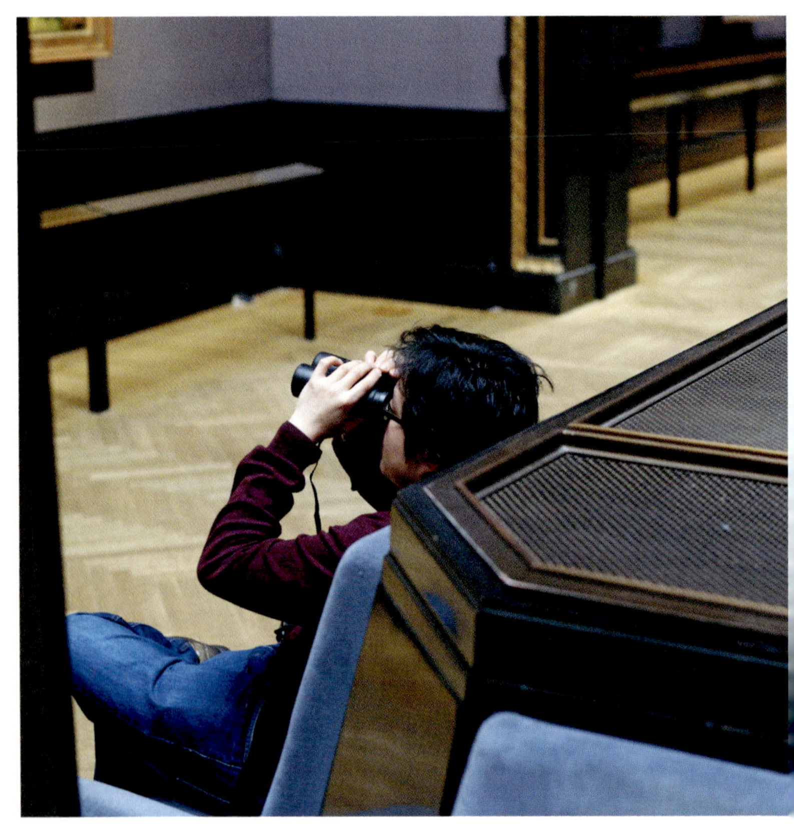

Kunsthistorisches Museum, Vienna

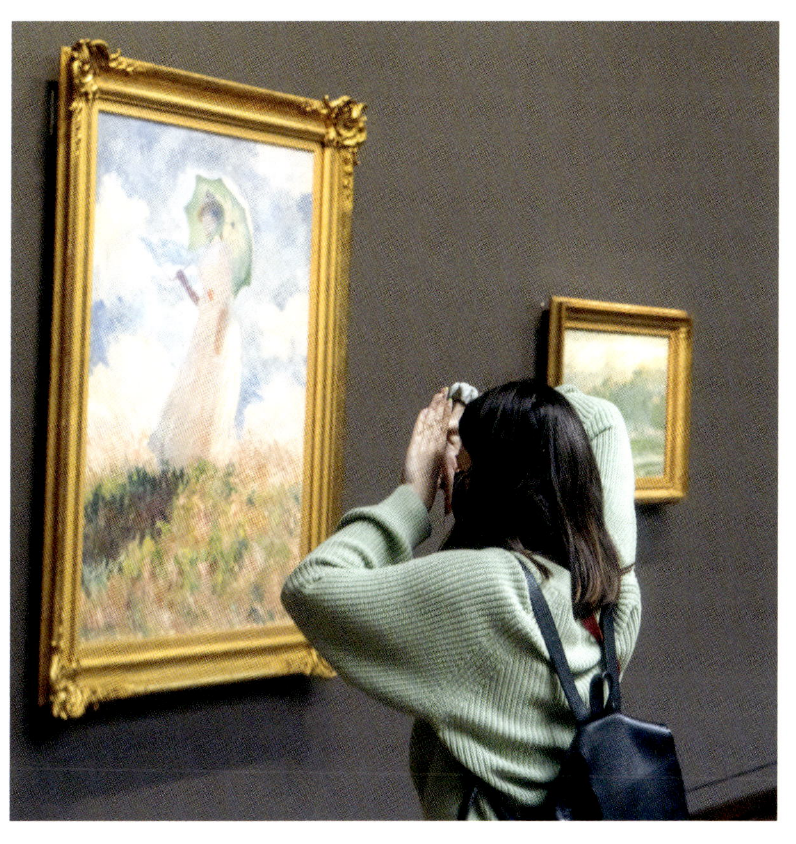

Monet, Musée d'Orsay, Paris

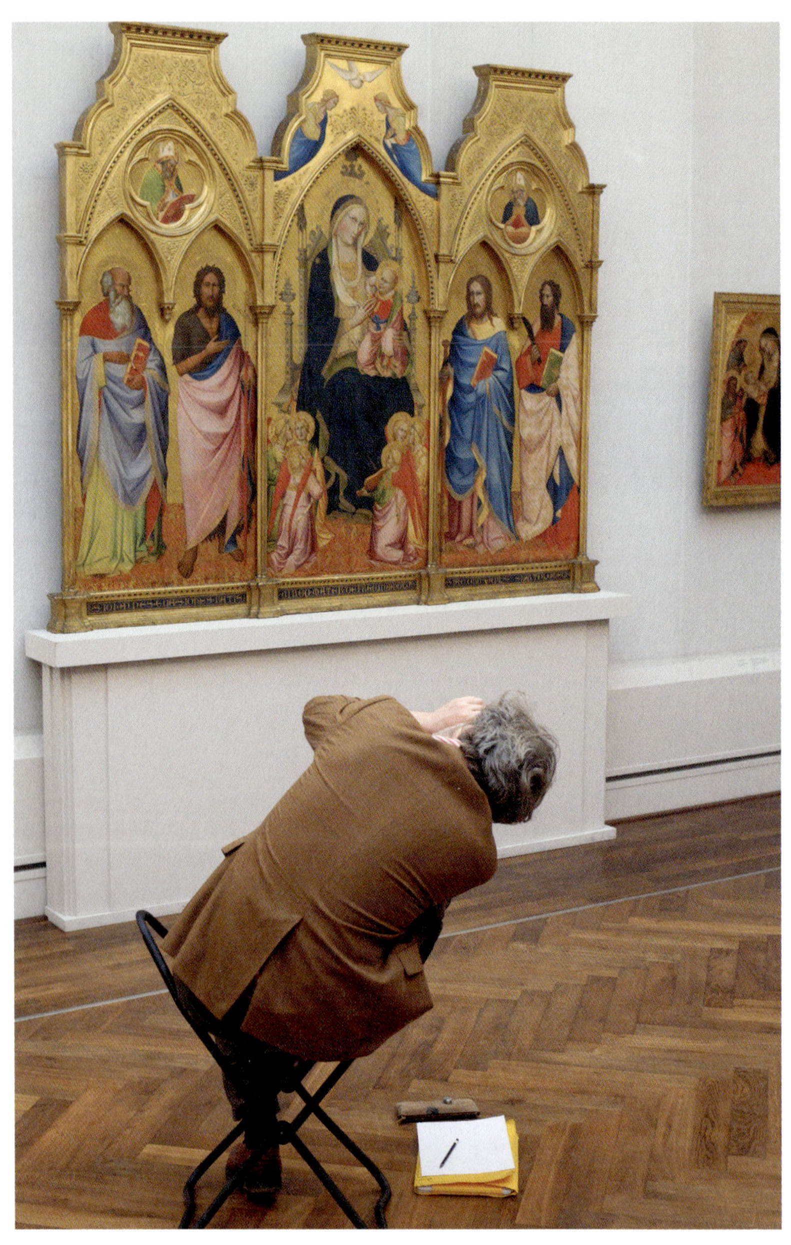

Gaddi, Gemäldegalerie, Berlin

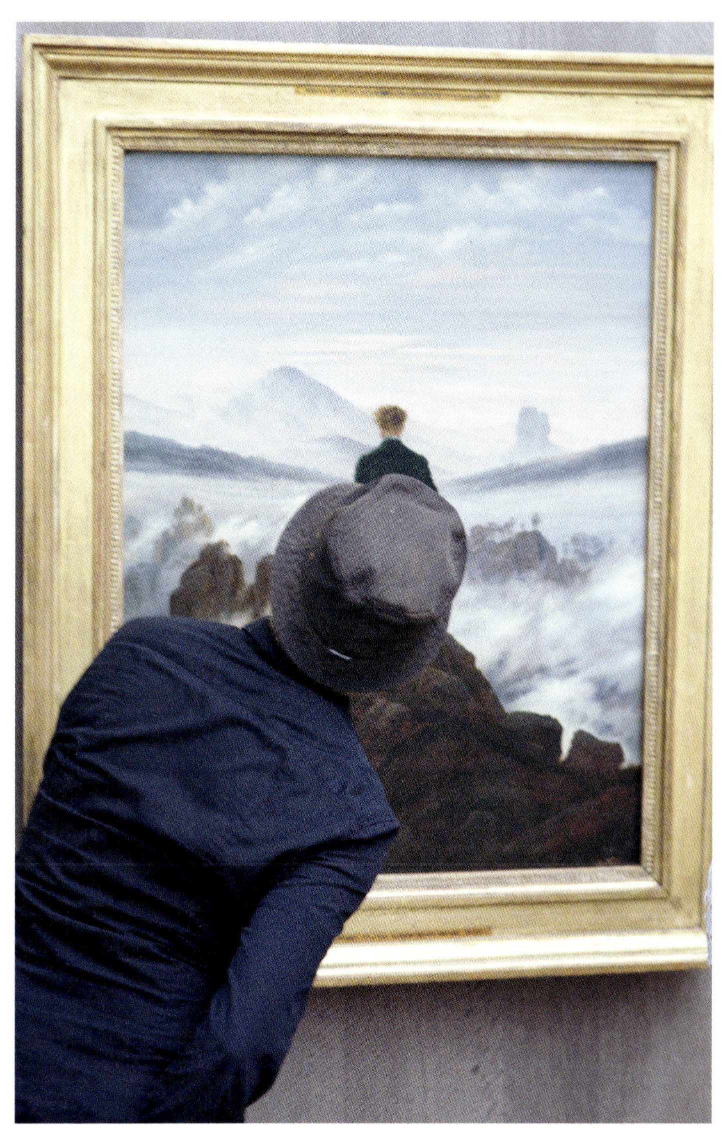

Friedrich, Alte Nationalgalerie, Berlin

MUSEUMS OF DEVOTION 2016–2021

Devotion is a special, perhaps the oldest, form of concentrated contemplation of art. Many works of art that are displayed in museums today were originally created as objects of devotion. Their powerful effect seems to transcend the boundaries of time and culture.

Devotion – Hingabe, Ergebenheit – ist eine besondere, vielleicht sogar die älteste Form der Kunstbetrachtung. Viele Kunstwerke, die heute in Museen gezeigt werden, sind ursprünglich als Gegenstand der Andacht entstanden. Ihre beeindruckende Wirkung entfalten sie offenkundig über die Grenzen von Epochen und Kulturen hinweg.

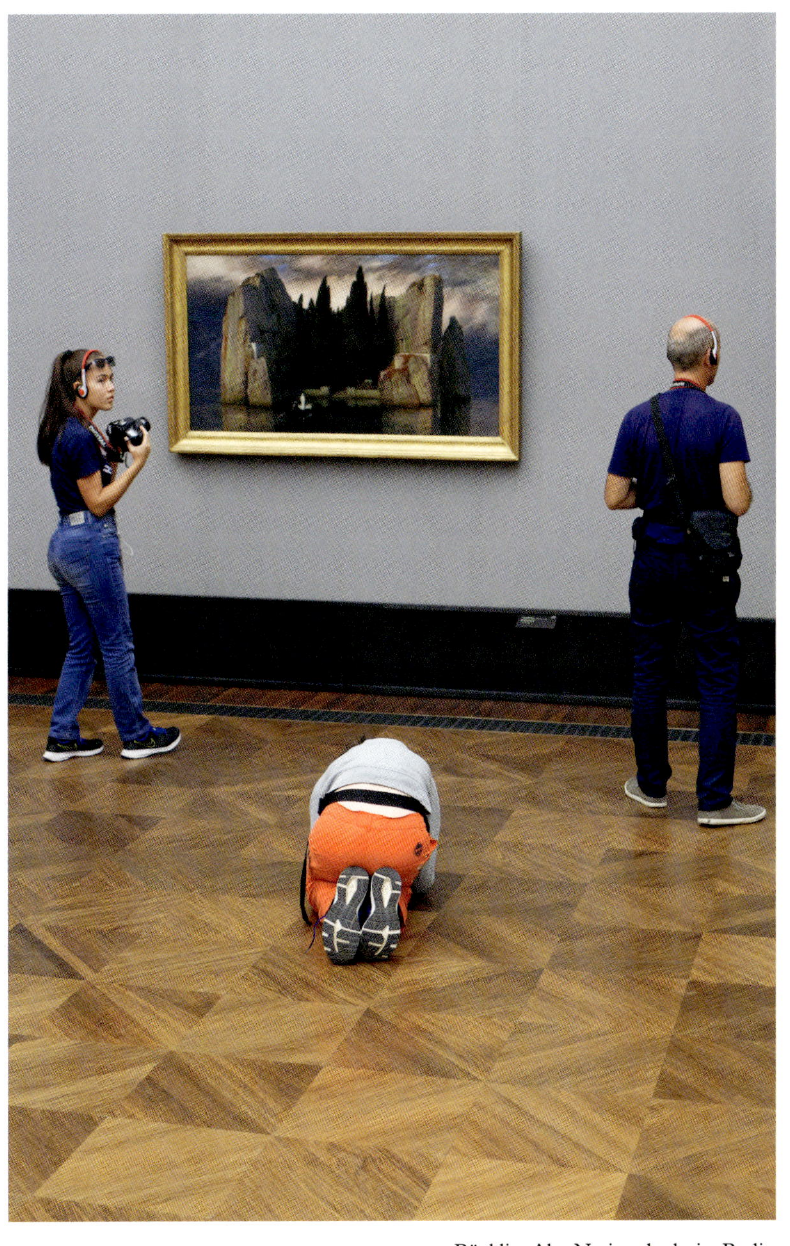

Böcklin, Alte Nationalgalerie, Berlin

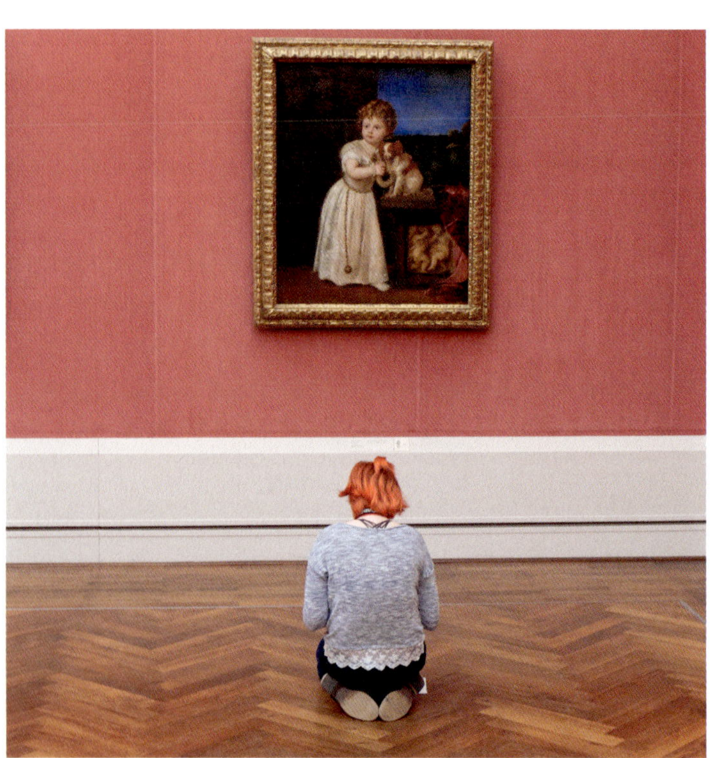

Titian, Gemäldegalerie, Berlin

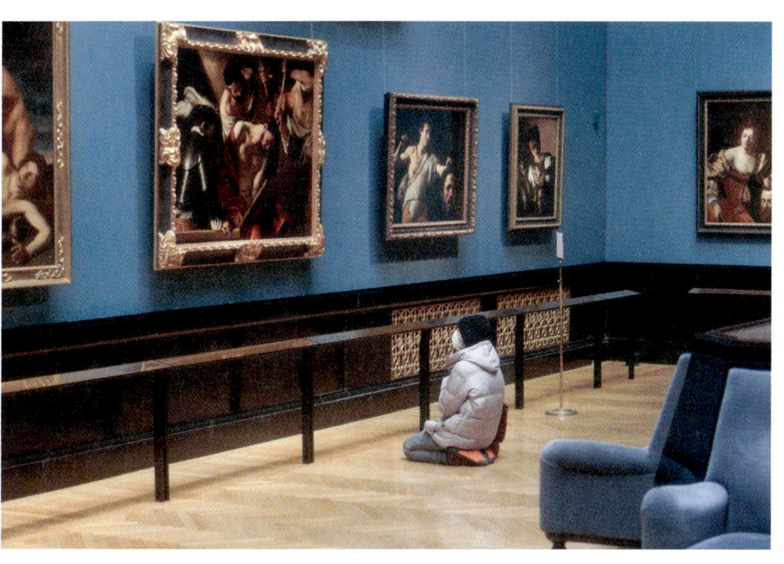

Caravaggio, Kunsthistorisches Museum, Vienna

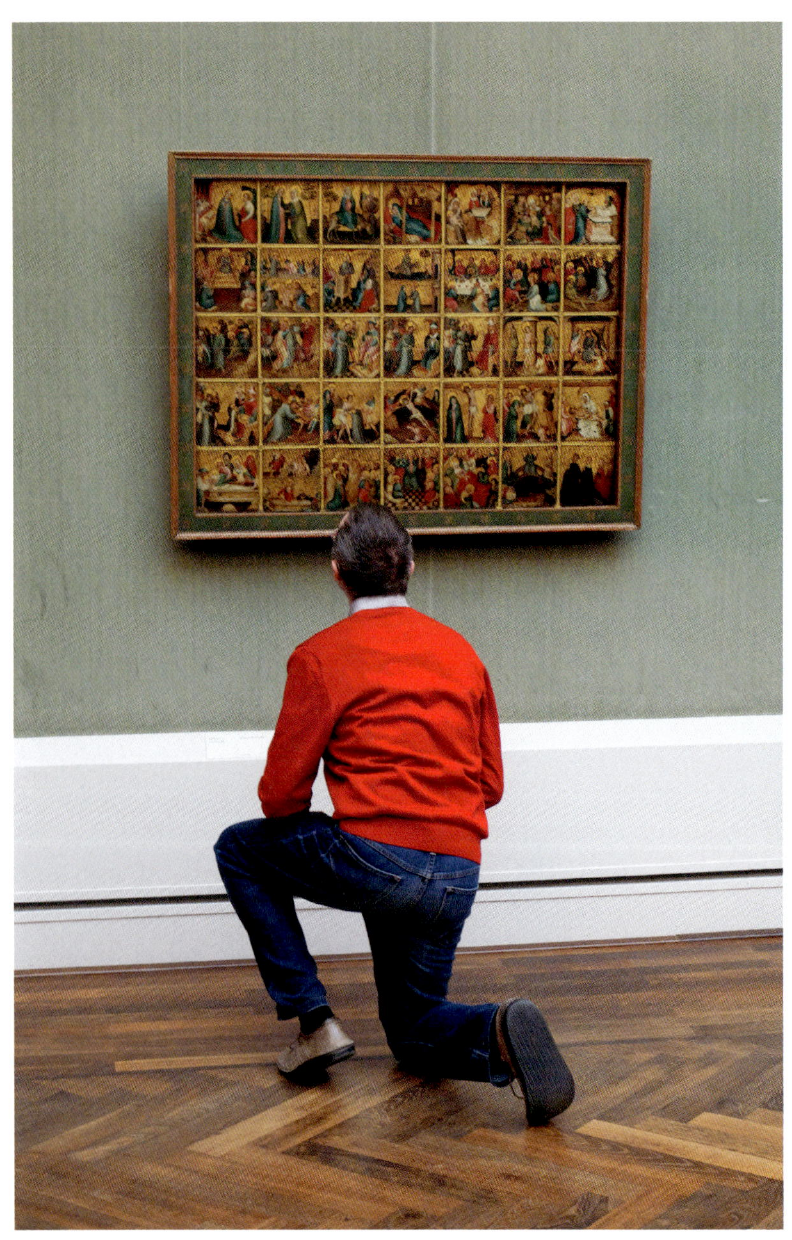

Gemäldegalerie, Berlin

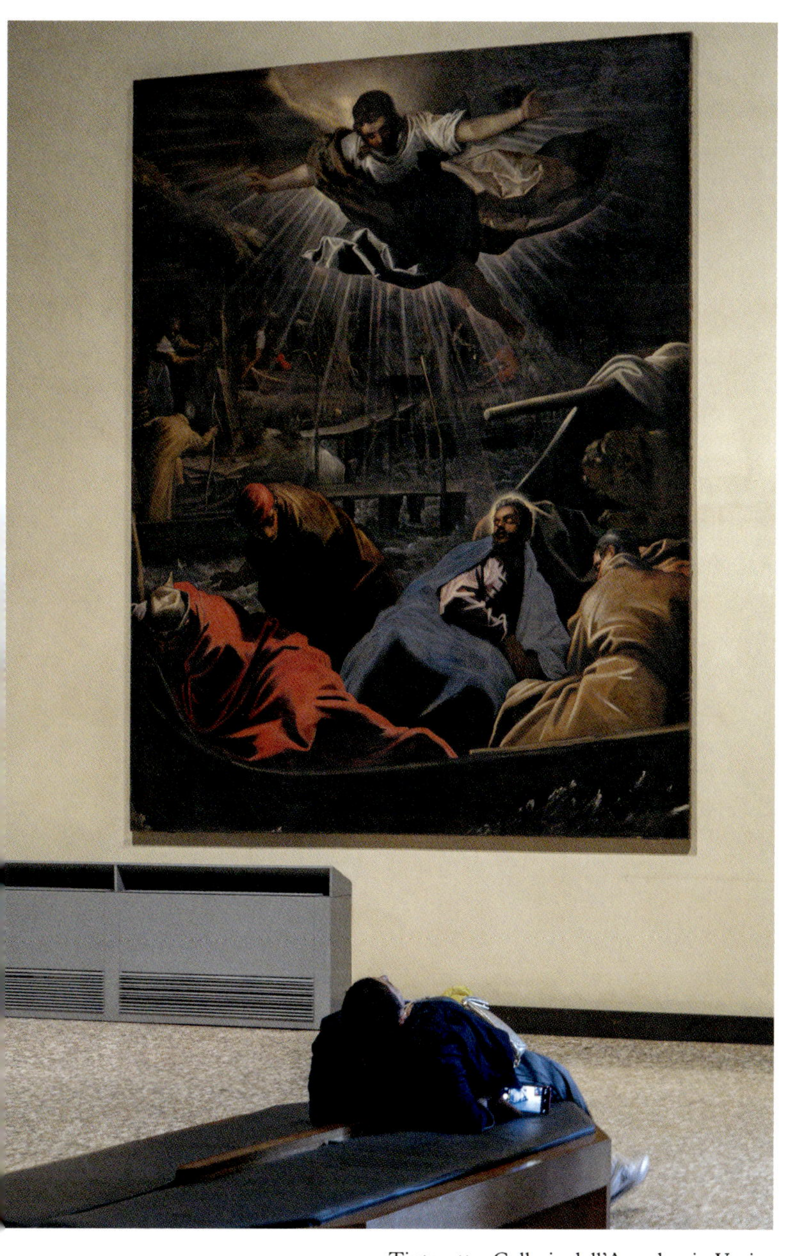

Tintoretto, Galleria dell'Accademia, Venice

READ
ING

2016–2021

As a photographer, Stefan Draschan is first and foremost a producer of images in the age of visual culture. In his self-portrayals as a reader, he celebrates the written word in print media and texts from Anaïs Nin to Helmut Berger in unusual settings, such as on the stairs of the Villa Malaparte. Here, he shares a love of bicycle culture with the former owner Curzio Malaparte.

Als Fotograf ist Stefan Draschan vor allem ein Produzent von Bildern im Zeitalter der visuellen Kultur. In seinen Selbstinszenierungen als Leser feiert er das geschriebene Wort in Printmedien und Texten von Anaïs Nin bis Helmut Berger in ungewöhnlichen Settings, etwa auf der Treppe der Villa Malaparte. Mit dem ehemaligen Besitzer Curzio Malaparte verbindet ihn die Liebe zur Fahrradkultur.

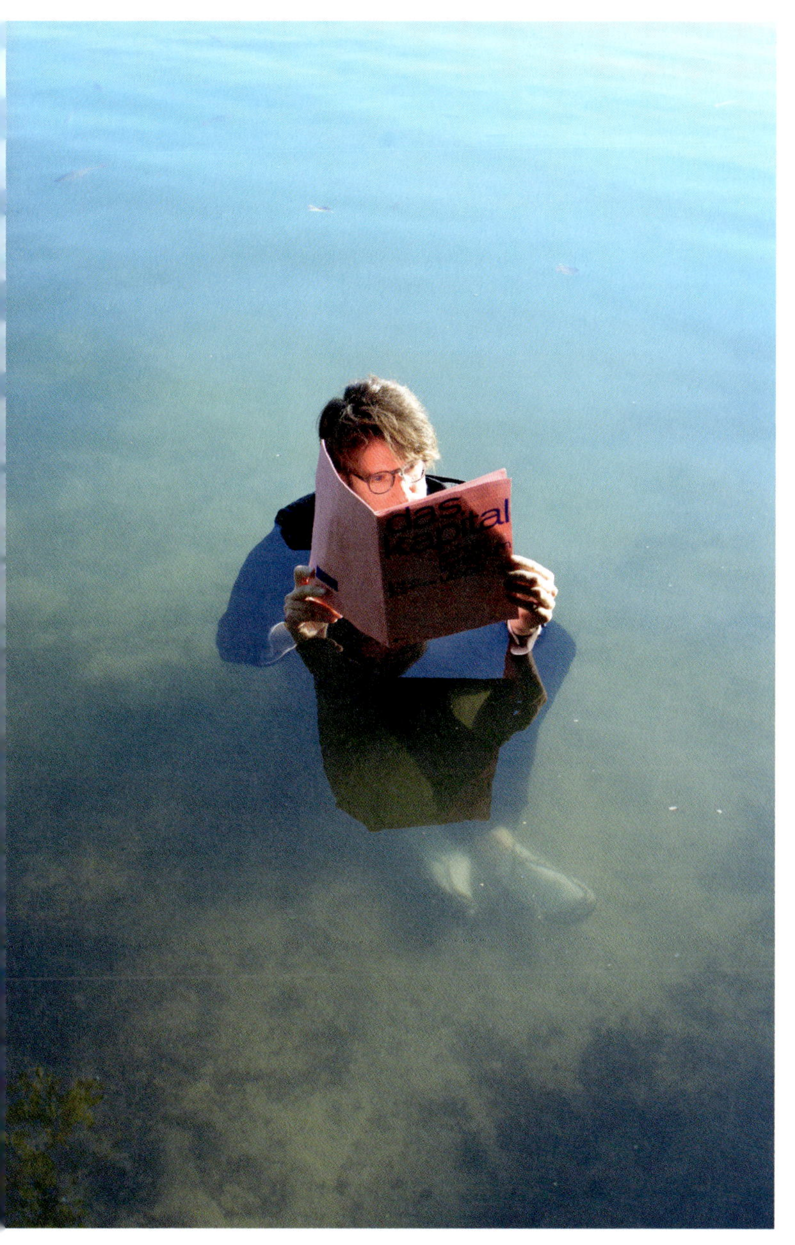

Das Kapital/Hamburger Bahnhof, Liepnitzsee/Brandenburg

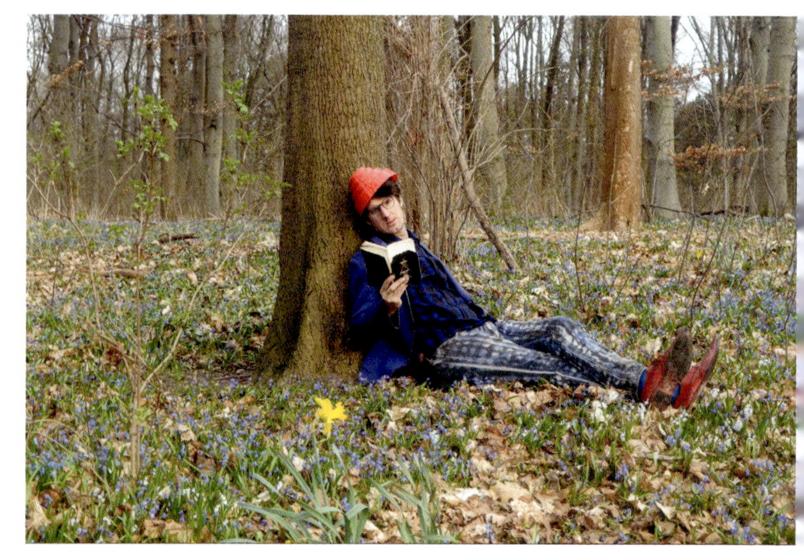

Nin, Berlin

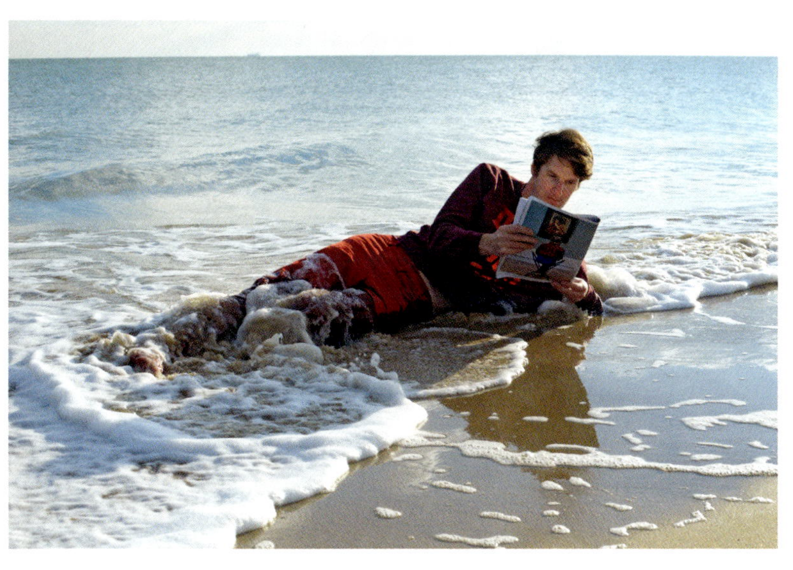

Süddeutsche, Île de Ré

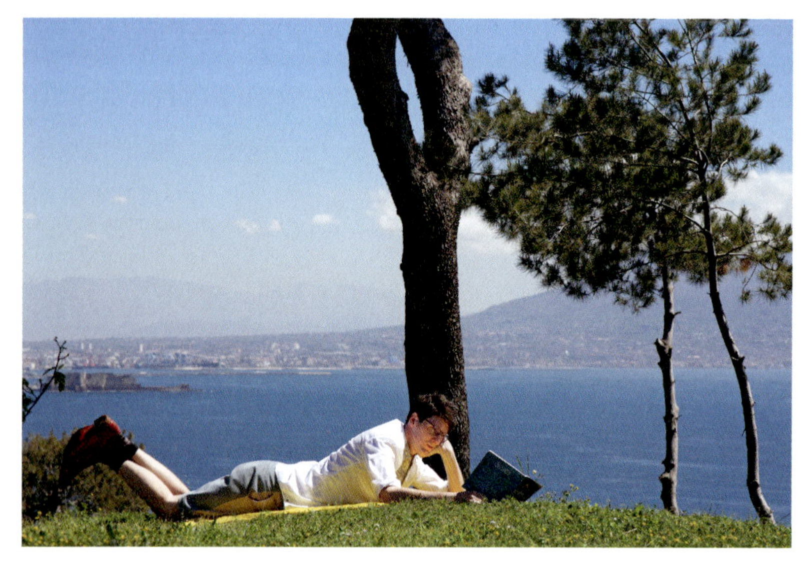

Coincidences, Naples

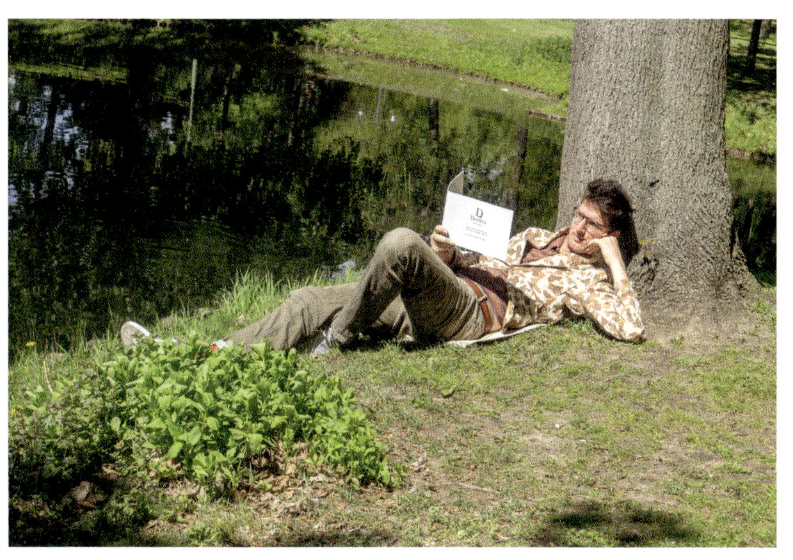

Hotel Domina Novosibirsk, Berlin

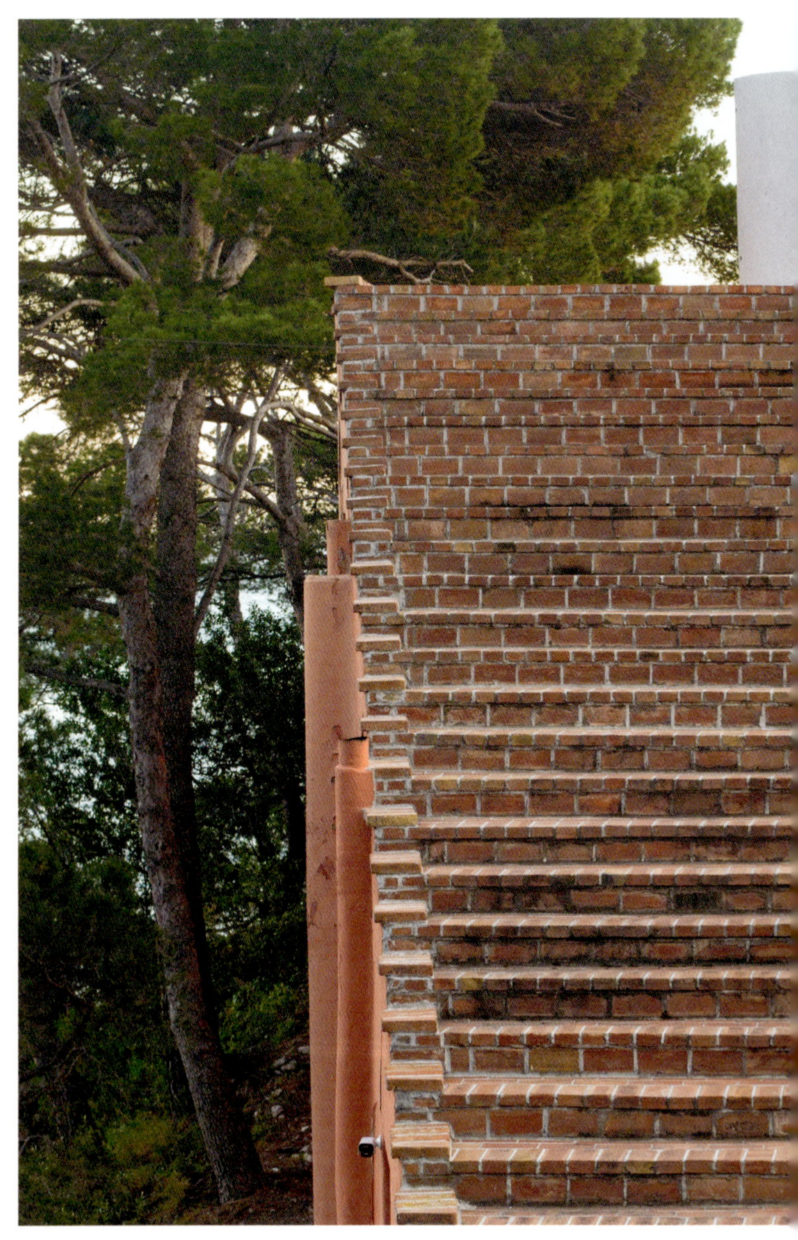

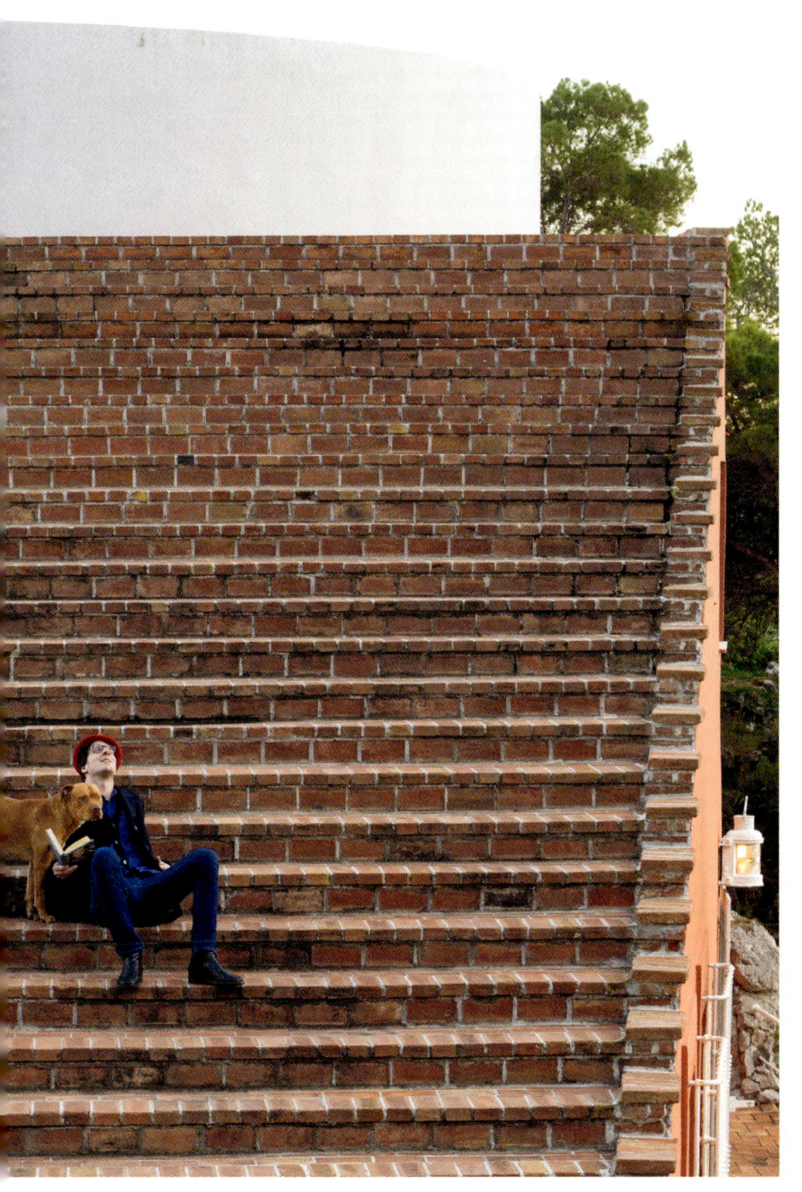

Helmut Berger, Capri

BICYCLE CULTURE

2015–2021

Stefan Draschan is not only a photographer, but also a bicycle activist. In his self-portrayals as a cyclist, he creates monuments to this pioneering form of transportation throughout Europe. As a "living sculpture," he triumphs over obstacles of all kinds, including tractors and wrecked cars, fossils of the fossil fossil fuel age.

Stefan Draschan ist nicht nur Fotograf, sondern auch Fahrradaktivist. In seinen Selbstinszenierungen als Radfahrer setzt er dieser zukunftsweisenden Form der Fortbewegung Denkmäler in ganz Europa. Als „lebende Skulptur" triumphiert er über Hindernisse aller Art, darunter auch Traktoren und Schrottautos, Fossilien des fossilen Zeitalters.

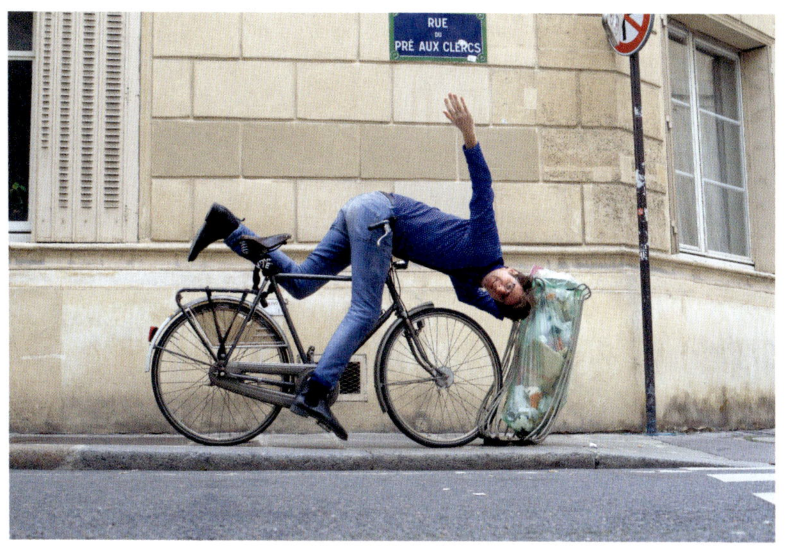
RUE
DU
PRÉ AUX CLERCS

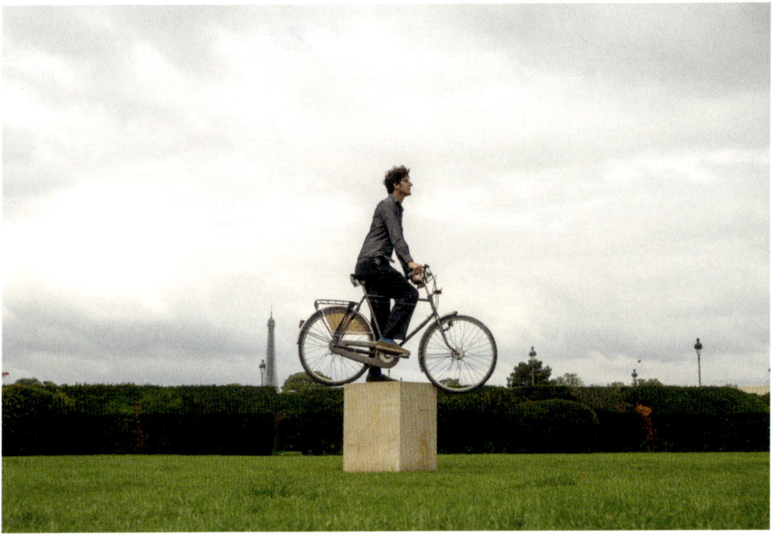

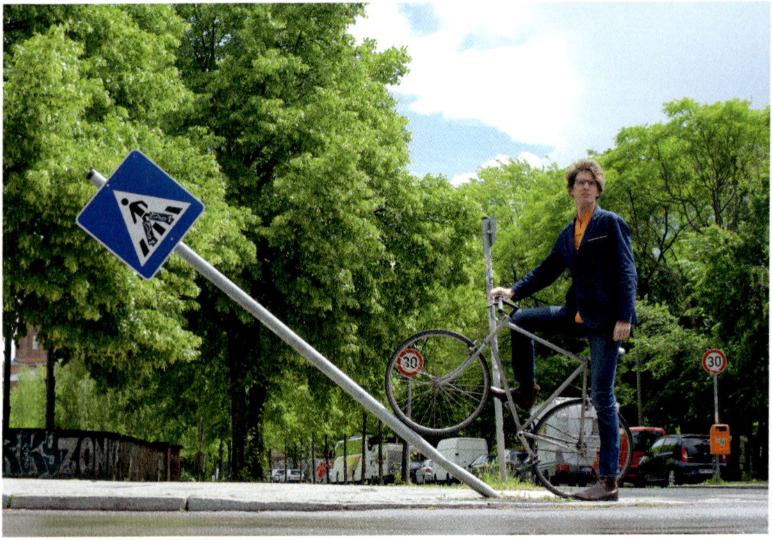

Paris | Berlin

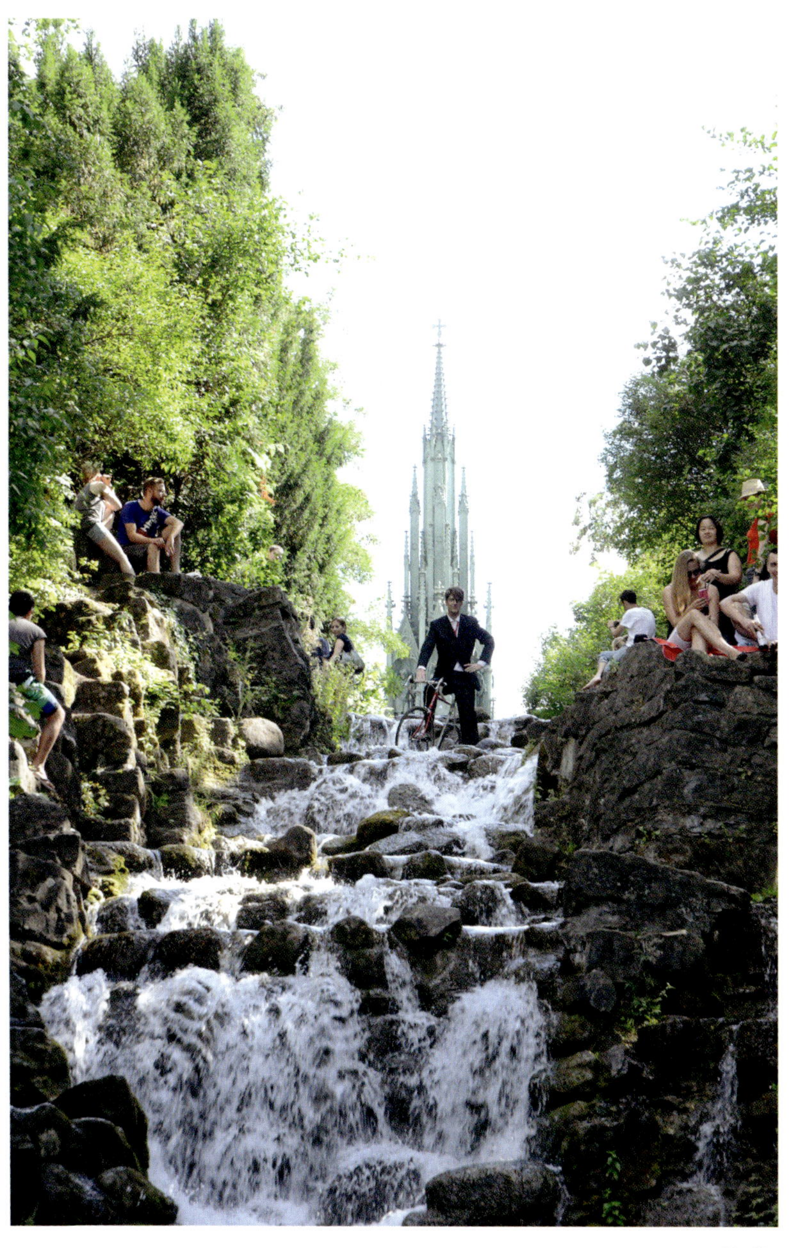

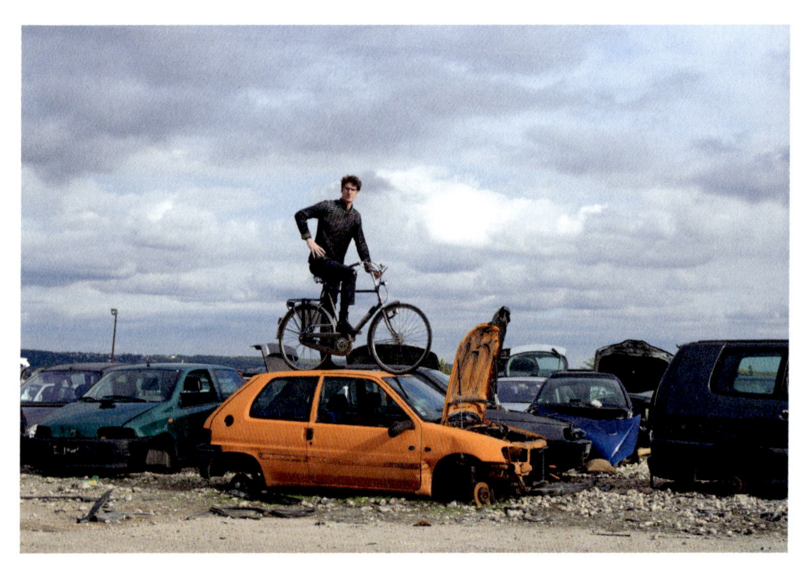

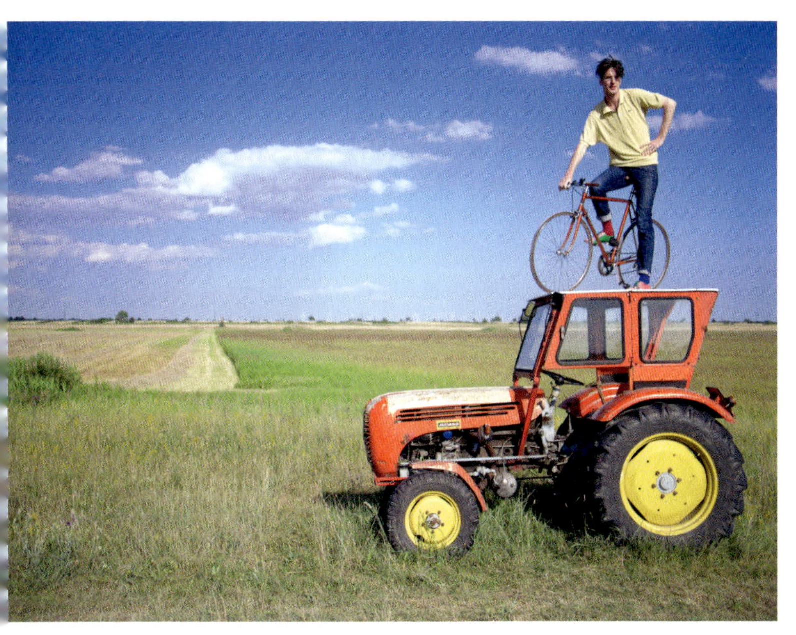

Burgenland

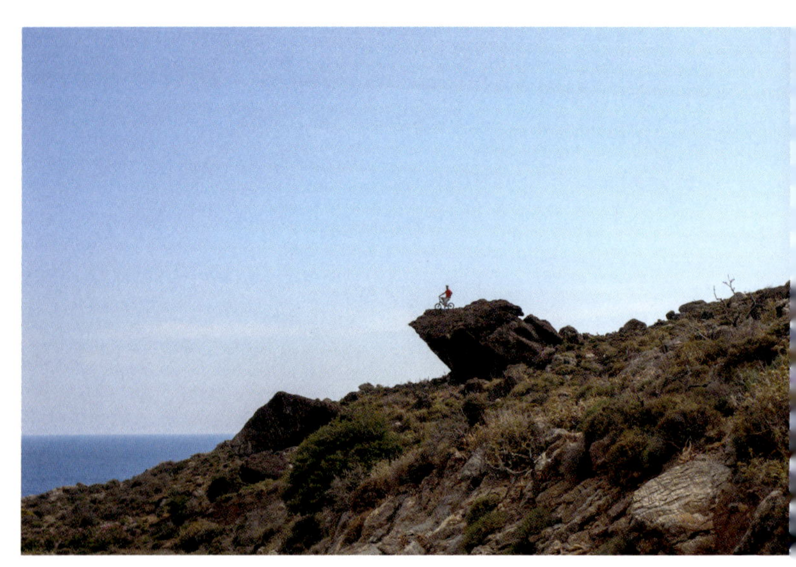

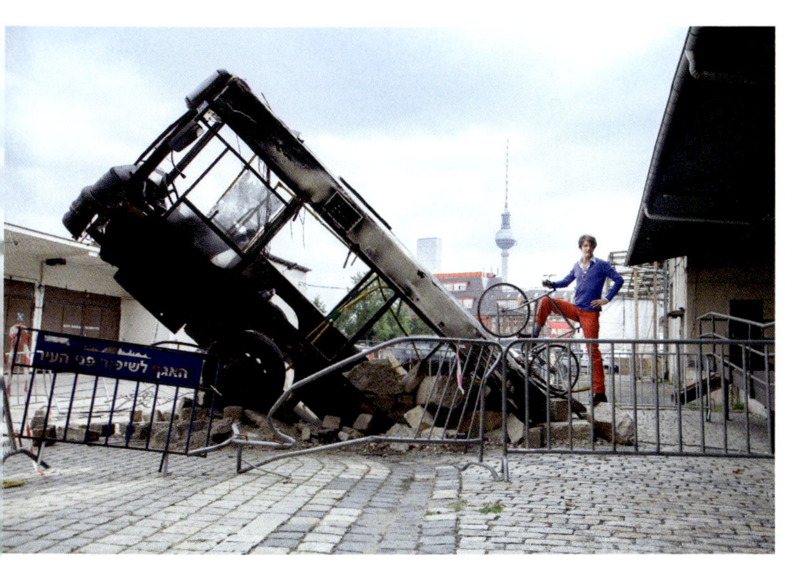

Text: Barbara Hess
Project management: Juliane Eisele, Hatje Cantz
Translation: Gérard Goodrow
Copyediting (English): Adam Jackman, Hatje Cantz
Graphic design: Rutger Fuchs Amsterdam
Production: Alise Ausmane, Hatje Cantz
Reproductions: Longo AG, Bozen
Printing and binding: Livonia Print, Riga
Paper: Magno Volume, 130 g/m²

PUBLISHED BY
Hatje Cantz Verlag GmbH
Mommsenstraße 27
10629 Berlin
Germany
www.hatjecantz.de
A Ganske Publishing Group Company

ISBN 978-3-7757-5543-6
ISBN 978-3-7757-5751-5 (e-book)

Printed in Latvia

Cover image:
Cars Matching Homes, Berlin
Back cover image:
Reading (about) Courbet, Sylt 2017